Telling '

Writers in Residence

List of Contributors

Writers

Alison

Jim

Helen

Linda

Tori

Tony

Tutor/Editor

Sue Pierlejewski

Jacket design and execution

Peter Jones-Tsang

General Factotum/Teaboy

Stan Jones

Contents

Contents (continued)

Sea Glass

My art therapy class was held in a room above the Seagulls Rest Café. It overlooked the bay where the tide came in twice a day leaving debris strewn across the sand and left twice a day taking some of it back out.

The people in my class were very much like the tide, broken people who came in and cried and ranted and painted, spreading out the debris of their lives in front of themselves like beachcombers searching for a glint of treasure. After a time when the colours of their paintings changed from angry reds, or sad blues and greys to brighter more hopeful colours, and the treasure gradually outweighed the debris, they left again, their broken edges soothed and smoothed the same way the sea works its magic on glass, crafting the hard edges into something smooth enough to hold in the palm of your hand.

Not everyone left, some stayed clinging to the class, the way a drowning man would cling to a buoy, hoping to survive the battering of the ocean. I knew as soon as I saw Una that she was a stayer. She drifted into the room like a sea urchin, her messy halo of hair giving her an ethereal quality. Her slightly too big clothes gave her a look of stylish defiance that belied the hurt and vulnerability in her eyes.

She didn't speak or make eye contact that week or the next and I didn't comment when she pushed her easel to the back of the room. She painted the same picture each week, an angry black and red swirling abstract surrounding a black figure of a woman with what looked like a small baby.

On the third week she moved her easel forward a little, towards Seb. Seb had been coming to class for nearly a year now. A quiet young man who described his job as 'taming nature for the rich'. He would arrive in class smelling of freshly cut grass with an extra helping of soil under his fingernails. He was a gentle soul with a deep well of empathy for others, always the first to encourage or comfort. Goodness only knows how he turned out like that given his story.

Seb had learnt very early, at the age of 6 what sex was, courtesy of the guests at his father's weekly dinner parties. The trauma had made him an introverted child who was subsequently bullied throughout his school years, his only solace being music and painting. When he first came to class, he only used grey charcoal and his early pictures had been brutal. Lots of men with their heads cut off or large knives sticking into their hearts. The trauma and damage he had suffered would never leave him but with the help of the class and his weekly psychiatry sessions he was learning to rebuild his life and he had now progressed from charcoal to coloured paints. He had talent, that young man and it was wonderful to see beautiful landscapes dancing across his paper full of hope.

I could see a connection building between Una and Seb, a shy smile one week, a hello the next and gradually Una moved further into the room and settled herself next to Seb. The week that Seb asked her what her pictures were about was the week Una finally let go of her debris, spilling it out into the group like a tsunami. It washed over the room, more shocking because it had been so unexpected, the salty bitterness of her pain had been two years in the making, and it ran deep below the shoreline.

She had been living in Ireland, a student when her parents were killed in an attack abroad. She had spiralled into the deepest despair and had sought help at university for depression and anxiety. When she fell pregnant to one of her lecturers, he used his connections with social services to have the child taken from Una. With a history of mental health issues, Una was no match for the father with a steady job and a barren wife ready and willing to take care of the child. She had moved to England, bringing her sorrow and pain with her on the ferry and was trying to rebuild her life. As the weeks progressed Una became chattier, the vulnerability that surrounded her gradually giving way to a tentative confidence that came and went depending on her mood. She and Seb became firm friends and started competing over their art work as it became apparent how talented they both were.

They had been coming to class for so long I thought they would always be there, so I was shocked one week in late September when they didn't show up. They didn't come the next

2

couple of weeks either and as it was an optional part of their therapy it was not for me to contact them, much as I longed to. It was a Saturday afternoon in October when I saw them again. I had gone to the nearest town to run some errands. It was cold and crisp out. The leaves had given up their last desperate hold on life and were brown and crunchy underfoot. I went into the Copper Kettle café to get warm and that's when I thought I saw them through the window. I had to use a napkin to wipe the steam from the glass to check. It was definitely them, Una and Seb. They were walking along hand in hand, laughing together at the antics of some small children chasing each other around the village pond. There was no mistaking the change in Una, the glossy tamed hair and the red coat that fitted her well and stretched across the swell of her pregnant belly. I knew then they would never be back at class. The tide had turned for them, finally in their favour and they had each other to cling to now, their edges smoothed to match perfectly.

Message from Beyond

'Here we are then.' said Fred looking round at the passengers sat in the back of the large black car. In the silence, their faces were a mix of sombre and pale. 'Not quite the usual for a funeral' he thought as he turned back to the steering wheel. They had arrived at the rugged, aged chapel in the large grounds of the old Victorian cemetery. Fred was not familiar with this particular chapel. It looked in need of a programme of modernisation and repair, unlike the other three or four ecclesiastical type buildings scattered over the large burial grounds.

Fred was used to doing all sorts of car runs, pickups and drops offs. He always ensured that his car was washed, waxed, and highly polished and presented to the highest standard – his standard. Important business travellers, mourners at funerals and whoever else hired the car didn't want to see scuffs, scratches, or dents on display, just something that he liked to think, in his words, 'looked the part'.

Fred had worked for over thirty years in the car industry. He was a chemist by profession and had been involved in car wash products, sweet smelling, highly foaming potions. They were exactly what customers had wanted when they put their much-loved vehicles through the car wash. Fred's work had been successful, and he had achieved much before his retirement three years ago. He used to say that he had started work as a six-foot-tall skinny lad with a mop of black hair and had ended a short, grey plump chap of aged years.

On retirement, wanting to have some casual occupation, Fred had started out as a freelance driver, working sometimes for the funeral business and sometimes for general chauffeur hire, for organisations and personal jobs. This suited him as he could choose his hours, decide which customers to take on and keep his interest in the auto business.

Fred glanced at his passengers through the rear-view mirror noting their inertia. A thought occurred to him that this was an unusual booking as each of the four passengers had been picked up individually at different locations across town. Usually, passengers were collected from one booking spot.

The first passenger, Tony, had been picked up from outside the Town Hall. He was a tall middle-aged man, with dark, short, cropped hair and a patterned handkerchief placed in the top pocket of his jacket. He had climbed into the car carefully, sliding across the dark red leather seat and gently fastening the black seatbelt into its chrome hold. He smelt of aftershave and Fred wondered if his pristine appearance suggested that he didn't get out much. Fred had tried to make conversation, but Tony was clearly not the talkative type and so Fred had given up and left him to his own thoughts.

Fred's next stop was to pick up his second passenger, Alec, from the Army Veterans' Hub. Typical of a military man, Alec had arrived promptly and was waiting as Fred arrived. He was striking in his military blazer fashioned with his regimental badge and other military regalia. His hair was receding, and it was greased back in place. He was a short tubby man with a ruddy complexion.

'Morning all' he said as he climbed into the car, bottom first and then swinging his legs in. 'Bloody hell, Tony, what are you doing here?'

'Alec' acknowledged Tony with a nod before turning to look out of the window.

'God, I need a drink. Whisky, a pint, anything – is it too early?' There was no response. Alec gave up and turned his head to look out of the window.

The car proceeded at a gentle pace as town was now becoming busy with shoppers and the last of the early morning commuting traffic. The engine hummed as the car climbed a hill up towards the centre heading to the finance area of town. The next pick up was from outside the Tax Office.

Harry was waiting, leaning on the wall. He looked like he had just got up out of bed and was looking around, surveying the area nervously as if it was unfamiliar. He climbed into the car and nodded towards his fellow passengers. 'Alec, Tony, yeah. Good to see you. How you doing?'

'Glad to be here, I think.' Alec replied. Tony remained silent, starring at Harry who sat opposite him 'terrible circumstances though'.

'Most unfortunate' muttered Harry.

'Are you all in, ready to move?' asked Fred looking at his three seated passengers. He took their silence to mean that they were ready, and the car moved on, the silence only broken by the purring of the engine.

Fred's final call was at the local library, on the edge of town. He managed to pick up some speed along the dual carriageway en route. He slid the privacy glass across, closing the interior window that separated the back of the car from the front, allowing the passengers to talk without being overheard or interrupted. He could hear murmurings every now and again; gentle conversation mixed with some apparent arguments amid the long silences.

Heading up to the library, Fred realised, too late, that the train barrier was down and there was a long queue ahead. Stuck in the line of cars, he tapped his fingers anxiously on the wheel as he waited, impatient. Fred hated to be late for his clients.

There was no one waiting outside the library, so Fred took the opportunity to turn the car round ready for a quick departure, as time was moving on. As he pulled the handbrake, a tall thin man, aged about sixty, approached the car. He was wearing thick, dark rimmed glasses which contrasted with his light grey suit. This was baggy against his slight frame and his hands shook as he tried to open the car door. It took him several attempts to unfasten the chrome handle before bending stiffly to climb in, seating himself next to Harry.

'Alright?' he asked and held out his trembling hand to shake it with each of the passengers. 'Long time, no see. Ha ha…what you been doin'?'

'This and that, a bit of the other. You know how it is, Lou' said Alec and laughed. The laugh reached through the privacy glass and Fred looked back at his passengers. He wasn't certain that he liked this pick up, but he reassured himself with the thought that he didn't have long to go with them now, and it was a very well-paid booking.

Amidst further bursts of conversation and mumblings the final stretch of the journey was soon complete, and the car pulled up slowly at the old chapel.

Fred watched calmly as the passengers climbed out. They didn't wait for one another but walked alone up to the old, weather beaten wooden framed door at the front of the building and entered. Fred nodded to himself, glad to be free of them, and putting the car into gear slowly drove away.

Lou was the first one into the chapel followed by Alec who had marched towards the door briskly. Harry was next and Tony ambled in last. The door banged shut behind them, disturbing the enveloping quietness of the old chapel, startling the birds nesting in the rafters.

It was dimly lit and cavernous, having little decoration. There were cracks in the once peach-coloured paintwork and plaster peeling where damp had penetrated the high walls.

The four men sat down, close to one another on the hard wooden benches, the remains of old cushioned kneelers tripping them up as they settled.

At the back of the chapel, already seated and unacknowledged by the group, two other mourners, both men in dark coats sat quietly. Piped music started to play, continuing for several minutes before a tall, middle aged blonde-haired woman arrived, dressed in a dark, fitted suit with a pair of smart black loafers and thick black tights. Her hair was tied up tightly and she was holding a file which she carried with an air of confidence.

Standing at the front, she introduced herself as Ann and briefly said she was here to conduct a very special but brief service for the lately deceased, Terry. She explained that first she would read out a note that he had left.

Removing a sheet of paper from her file she began to read, speaking clearly. 'Welcome Lou, Tony, Alec and Harry. Well, who'd have thought it... me going before you lot.' She paused and the four 'mourners' looked at one another. Lou was trembling more than ever as his hand rested on the top of the chair in front of him. Tony stared into space and Alec and Harry glanced at one another.

Ann continued to read, 'That job, how long ago was it? You never forgave me, did you? I had to, though, those poor sods that

you hurt. Anyway, I knew one of you would come after me…
you know who you are, which one of you it was.' Ann paused,
taking a deep breath.

'You never forgave me for reporting you, did you? I couldn't
stop myself, despite the money you gave me. I thought you'd
come after me once you were out. Watch your backs, guys, you
can't trust one another. At least one of you or more saw me off.
I'll give you a little time to work it out, perhaps.' Ann had
finished reading and quickly stepping away from the wooden
lectern, turned round and disappeared through an open door that
promptly slammed shut behind her.

Harry was open mouthed and turned to Alec 'Who the hell
was she? Supposed to be a memorial for Terry, not a bloody wind
up'.

'How long have you been out, Al?' Lou asked Alec.

'About six months' replied Alec

'And you?' Lou asked, turning to Harry.

''Bout the same, maybe three maybe four months' was the
turgid reply.

'Tony, you've been out for longer, haven't you?'

Tony didn't reply but lowered his head. He started to sob, and
his body shook. words clearly frightened.

'I'm off, I bloody well need that drink' said Alec 'let's get
back to the car.' He stumbled his way over the kneelers and the
knees of the others as he made to leave.

Lou stood up, taking his dark, thick set glasses off his head,
holding them in his shaking right hand.

'Terry, you idiot. You're dead. You can't get us anymore' he
shouted starring at some imaginary figure ahead of him 'Where's
that woman anyway? She's got some explaining to do'.

'I'm scared' cried Tony, 'scared of you all. I didn't do it'.

'We gave Terry half of the cash we stole because we needed
it hiding.' Alec said.

'Terry only told Sergeant Jacks and I never understood why
the Sergeant didn't get his superiors to get Terry sent down with
us. Where did his alibi come from? That proof of 'innocence' and
no involvement'

'Yeah, yet he kept the bloody money' said Lou 'sure he …'

Two shots rang out, followed immediately by two more. The two men seated at the back of the Chapel moved forward to clear up their work and leave with the evidence. Easy to carry out coffins from a chapel. They had done their job.

The door by the lectern re-opened and in came Ann. She walked over to the main Chapel door and turned the old cast iron key in the lock, leaving it in the door where it belonged.

The gang of four now gone, Ann Jacks (retired Sergeant) could continue to live off the proceeds she had shared with her Partner, Terry. Terry had always been grateful for the alibi she had given him. The two of them knew that the guys, or at least one, would come after him, once they were out. They had planned what Ann would have to do next.

Fred was part of Ann's plan. He had driven her to events when she was a Sergeant and for years after. She knew that when she told him that no waiting was required and to leave the Chapel as soon as he had dropped the four men off, he would and, without question, would suspect nothing.

The Survivor

Kate looked out of her kitchen window at the cherry blossom tree. The overnight wind had scattered its fragile blossom, leaving only the memory of its beauty behind. Its transience was part of its appeal for Kate.

Behind her the kettle began to sing, its tone mournful as she lifted it from the hob. After a few minutes Kate poured almost boiling water on to the coffee grounds. Whilst she waited for it to settle before pressing the plunger down, she reached for her favourite mug - hand painted with a picture of an oyster catcher. It had been a farewell gift from her closest friend, now 12,000 miles away living the good life in a remote part of her native New Zealand. She added a lump of sugar to sweeten the strong black coffee. BC – before cancer – she used to joke that she only had sugar in coffee on really bad days. There had been more than her fair share of those in recent times.

Returning to the window to drink her coffee, Kate knocked on the glass in hopes of scaring next door's ginger tom away. He had taken to using her back garden as his toilet. The cat stared at her with insolent eyes. Slowly, very slowly, he turned his back on her and sauntered down the path, making sure that she knew it was his choice to leave, not hers.

Glancing at the clock Kate realised she had better get a move on if she was to meet her sister and niece as planned at the garden centre. She was hoping to get some ideas for summer planting, maybe buy a garden ornament, something to deter the cat, perhaps even think about new garden furniture for when the weather turned warmer.

Kate took some sausages from the freezer. With jacket potatoes and beans that was the simple meal she planned to cook for the three of them. It would be the first time she had entertained in over two years thanks to covid, cancer and chemotherapy. At least the oven didn't need cleaning she congratulated herself.

Kate picked up a carrier bag, containing a wig, worn more to please others distressed by her hair loss as a result of

10

chemotherapy, than for herself. She added a brand-new pair of black patent leather shoes, an almost instantly regretted impulse online buy during lockdown. Some days parcel deliveries were the only human contact she'd had in the dark times when she was shielding. Hopefully, the charity shop would get some benefit. She gave herself a final once over in the hall mirror and saw reflected back a tall, willowy, smartly dressed woman in her early fifties, the new elfin haircut still a surprise. Checking that she had her keys and phone, Kate locked the door behind her and set off, enjoying the, never again to be taken for granted, feel of fresh air on her face. Perhaps she would drink her coffee without sugar tomorrow.

Where There's a Will...

Nellie, yawned, stretched, and looked around the bedroom that had been hers since her long gone childhood. Faded flowery patterned wallpaper, a musty smell, and an old oak wardrobe, all of which mirrored her life, plain, dull and uninteresting. Not for her a life of luxury she thought grimly.

A strident voice cut through her musings. 'Nellie, where's my tea?'.

'Coming mother.' was all she could manage as she wrapped her thin dressing gown round her even thinner shoulders, and shuffled down stairs, feeling the threadbare carpet beneath her feet, just as the post dropped through onto the worn Welcome mat on the floor.

Nellie stared at the small pile of envelopes on the mat and didn't rush to pick it up, resigned to receiving nothing but bills and circulars, never any personal post. Nellie and Mother had few friends and no relatives, so there were never any postcards or family letters to look forward to.

She took Mother her tea, and two plain biscuits, a morning routine which had been ongoing since her father died ten years ago. Mother's bedroom was larger than Nellie's but shared the same flowery faded wallpaper. There was a small washbasin in one corner, a Lloyd loom chair with a cushion matching the wallpaper, and on the bedside table, a picture of her looking slim and pretty with a tall handsome man, Bill, her husband, on their wedding day. Their happy smiling faces beamed out from the faded back and white photo, the excited anticipation of their new life together leaping out. There must have been a time when Mother was happy, Nellie thought to herself, as she put the tray of tea down, carefully moving the picture. She looked down on this frail woman lying in the bed, no sparkle in the dull eyes, and a mouth that curled downwards giving her face a permanent disapproving look.

Returning to the kitchen she picked up the post from the mat and poured herself a cup of strong coffee, thumbing through the envelopes lazily. As she had thought, the post was all junk mail. Except for a plain brown envelope addressed to her. Nellie sipped her coffee and stared at the envelope. It was definitely addressed to Miss Nellie Burton. She felt her pulse rate quicken. Who could be sending her an official looking letter? It was from Dunwoody and Smithers, a local firm of solicitors. The letter asked her to get in touch with them urgently, as they had some information which would be of interest to her. What did that mean? Of interest to her? Sounded like she was going to benefit from something ….

Or was it a scam…. not that Nellie knew much about scams though she'd heard about them. Her first reaction was the same as most people…. don't believe it. Throughout her thirty-one years she had learned never to expect anything good to happen, and then you wouldn't be disappointed.

But something told her to ignore her suspicions and, as the letter implied urgency, she picked up the phone and dialled the number. The bright voice of the receptionist that answered quickly assured Nellie that the letter was genuine. An appointment was made for her to meet Mr. Dunwoody, senior partner no less, the following morning.

Meanwhile Nellie allowed herself the luxury of daydreaming about what the news might be. That she was really the abandoned daughter of a wealthy prince who had returned to rescue her from her miserable life? Or that a far distant relative had died and left her a £1,000,000! The first dream was unrealistic, she knew that. The second dream, whilst extravagant in the amount, held the possibility of another life. A life where she could do things, achieve things for herself, far away from here. She sighed and reminded herself, that with her luck, it was more likely that a distant relative had died and left a pile of debts, for which she was now responsible.

The next morning, Nellie was up and dressed even earlier than usual. She gave Mother breakfast and announced that she had to go into town.

'What do you need to go to town for? 'Mother, complained, annoyed at anything which would take Nellie away from her.

'Just some things I need to get, Mother. I'll be home by lunchtime '.

'Well, make sure you are', came the sharp reply.

13

Nellie rushed to escape and caught the next bus into town, so excited she left the bus one stop early by mistake. However, the short walk to the Solicitor's Office enabled her to regain her composure.

The office was situated in a tall grey concrete building, weather worn, surrounded by similar ugly sixties style edifices, worn at the edges, in need of some restoration or a simple good clean. She climbed the stairs from the street and pushed at the revolving door. The interior was dark, and as her eyes adjusted to the limited lighting, she could make out dark oak bookcases, desks, and padded chairs in the reception area. Everything she had imagined a solicitor's office would look like.

Her earlier excitement evaporated as the receptionist, having welcomed her with a smile, announced her arrival quietly on her intercom. Soon Mr Dunwoody appeared, introduced himself and invited her into his office.

'Cup of tea Miss Burton?' he smiled at her gently as she passed into his office.

'Err… just a glass of water please,' Nellie tried to quell the butterflies in her stomach.

Nodding to the listening receptionist who rose to answer Nellie's request, Mr Dunwoody closed the door and settled himself down behind his imposing desk. Nellie sat on the hard chair opposite.

'Miss Burton, I have a letter for you, so I will leave you for a few minutes so you can read it privately '

He handed Nellie a crumpled vanilla envelope with a reassuring smile and quietly left her alone. Nellie stared at the unfamiliar scrawl of her name on the envelope as she withdrew the single sheet of paper. In a daze she began to read:

'Nellie, This is the hardest letter I have ever had to write and will come as a bit of a shock to you. My name is Margaret Shepherd and I am your natural mother. I gave birth to you when I was a young woman of twenty-three. Your father and I fell in love but couldn't get married because he was already married. He couldn't or wouldn't leave his wife. I was in no position to bring you up by myself. Eventually your father told his wife about our affair, and together they agreed to bring you up as their own. I had to allow them to adopt you. Giving you up was the most difficult decision I have ever had to make, but it was made easier knowing that you were going to be with your father whom I knew would look after you well.

I left Salford because I couldn't bear the thought of seeing you, yet never being able to hold you. I went to college and studied hard, later receiving a mature student's grant to study medicine at university. I never looked for or found a man to replace your father. I chose instead to concentrate on my career. I became a surgeon, and later specialised in oncology, which as you may know is the treatment of cancer. Ironic really, as it is cancer which will ultimately take me. Which is why I am writing to you now. Until my diagnosis three years ago, I was the Senior Consultant at the Newton Hospital in Boughton, leading clinical trials into the treatment of bone cancer…the variant of cancer which is sadly killing me. Although I am now facing death, I am at peace. I can only hope that you have had a happy and fulfilled life and that you have felt loved and wanted. I want to let you know that I never stopped loving you, and that I think about you every day. My darling girl, even though we have never met, you are and always will be mine. My biggest regret is that we have never met, and that I never had the chance to watch you grow and flourish. I hope you can find it in your heart to forgive me for giving you up. Finally, I want to give you just one piece of advice. You can be, or do, anything you set your mind to. There are no barriers. Except self-belief, and if you don't have self-belief yet, just borrow it from someone else, until you have it.

I send you all my love and wish you a happy and successful life from here on. Your loving mother,

Margaret Shephard.

Nellie sat quietly, the letter unfolded in her lap as Mr Dunwoody entered the room.

'Any questions for me, my dear? I'm sure this has come as a bit of a shock to you'. 'I'm not sure…. I didn't…. I don't….'. Nellie sighed and shook her head. 'I know. It's a lot to take in. May I suggest you take some time to re-read the letter and digest it.'.

'But…my mother? … I didn't…I …' Nellie paused, straightening up.' Can I meet her?'

Mr Dunwoody shook his head, sadly. 'I'm afraid that Margaret died a few months ago.'

Nellie stared at him, her face pale. 'But…you had this letter…why…?

'I am sorry, Miss Burton, but I was under strict instructions that this letter was not to be given to you until after the funeral, and after probate had been granted. There is of course, a will, which we can read at your convenience. You are the sole beneficiary. Might I suggest we meet again in a few days' time?

'I think that would be a good idea 'Nellie mumbled, folding up the letter, and placing it carefully in her bag.

'Thank you'.

'Not at all. Please, make an appointment with the receptionist when you feel ready to come back.' Nellie nodded and, in a daze, stumbled out of the office, out of the building, down the steps to the busy pavement, narrowly avoiding bumping into the office workers rushing past her.

Reaching the bus stop she sank onto the hard plastic seat with gratitude, ignoring the annoyed stares of the pensioners hustling each other to also sit down. She struggled to comprehend what she had just learned. Now, looking back, things began to fall into place; the difficult relationship she had had with Mother all these years, the lack of love, she had always felt, especially since her father had died.

Her father, she remembered with love and affection, and Mother's coldness…now she could begin to understand. To accept another woman's child, and bring it up as her own, was an amazing thing to do.

Sitting on the bus Nellie re read the letter, wondering about the person Margaret had been, wondering how different her life might have been had she had this birth mother in her life. But this woman had followed her dreams. Whilst Mother had given up on her own dreams, forgiven her husband, and provided his lovechild with a safe and secure home. She began to look at Mother in a new light.

Home then and Nellie paused at the gate, looking up at the modest terraced house, the only home she had ever known and the front window behind which she knew Mother would be waiting for her. She nodded to herself and slowly inserted her key into the front door, deep in thought.

'Cup of tea, Mother? ', she called out, walking through to the kitchen. 'I'll put the kettle on. Thought we might go shopping later? Time for some new shoes, I think. For both of us.'

Lily

Lily opens her eyes, glancing down at her hands – no longer withered and feathery, riddled with arthritis and bent with pain and immobility, now they are beautifully manicured with smooth, soft skin, as she turns her head, her hair bounces on her shoulders – sleek and black, no longer wispy, lifeless, and thin. The last few years had been a blur for Lily – familiar sounds with unfamiliar faces, vague memories of being lost, the fear of being found and the confusion of not knowing. The loss of sensation until the dreams came and she could just 'be' again.

She wonders if this could be another dream, yet the breeze on her face and the smell of the flowers all feels so real. The way her skin brushes against the sway of her skirt. At last, she is pain-free, and Lily almost feels like she can fly. Distant memories of her last few days come flooding back – machines, beeping, injections, noise, pain and worried faces. Then an overwhelming sense of calm, this same feeling over-riding everything now. Taking a deep breath, she continues to step into the light.

His outline strikes her first before she hears his voice, the voice she knew so well that it was almost a part of her, until it wasn't.

'Lily I've been waiting for you'.

As her eyes refocus, Lily sees the man she fell in love with walking towards her, exactly as he was all those years ago when they first met, tall, tanned, handsome with a dazzling smile and eyes that sparkled wildly in the sun. Looking into his eyes as he approaches – she feels alive again, her heart fully mended, her mind sharp and her body vibrant.

Frederik was older than Lily, quite significantly so and her parents didn't welcome their courtship to begin with. But they knew that it would be difficult to stop their beautiful, headstrong daughter and so, at 17, Lily married Frederik in their local Church in South Manchester. There was nothing they could do but support her.

Their love was wild and passionate and despite the heartbreak of failing to conceive, they enjoyed 20 glorious years together.

Life was unpredictable, spontaneous and fun – full of music and laughter. Frederik worked as an actor – away from home a lot as he travelled to different theatres sharing his craft. Until his death, Lily worked part-time in a supermarket, the regular income helping support the household bills.

Looking over at Frederik now, her heart swells and her eyes water. The elation of seeing him again brings back the pain of when she lost him.

She thinks back to the day her world fell apart when her darling Frederik was taken from her in a tragic accident. She had been working and was called into the manager's office where the news was broken to her. She remembers the stale smell of cigarettes and damp that filled her lungs and the blue and orange rows of flowers on the wallpaper – she was so desperately trying to count to hold herself together. But it was no good, the news struck Lily like a ton of bricks, wiping out the very core of her, shattering her heart into tiny pieces like a vase that would never be the same again despite how carefully it was put back together.

And someone did try to mend her – dear Thomas who held her as she wept and taught her how to breathe again. In time, their friendship developed into love – strong and secure until Thomas too was taken from her life too early, after a long and defeated battle with cancer. She nursed him well, held him and sang to him while he endured the treatments that drained the colour from his skin and the sunshine from his soul. And then she knew it was time to let him go as she saw the life slip away from his withered body and peace wash over him. Thomas. The sound of his name in her mouth brings back memories – a mix of pain and love.

Thomas and Lily had enjoyed twenty-seven amazing years married together. Thomas gave Lily everything he could – a beautiful home and life and his heart. The kindness in his face shines through now, his eyes twinkling, and her body feels warm and safe again as she hears the familiar soothing voice saying,

'Lily, I knew we'd meet again' Did the sound of his name awaken his soul?

With the bright light shining from behind him, she can see that he is no longer thin and wasting, but once again the strong comforter he was when they first became a couple. Her heart is full of joy as he reaches out to her.

19

Lily glances from one silhouette to another, wondering if she'll have to make a choice between the man, she fell in love with so passionately all those years ago, or the man who saved her and put her life back together.

She reaches out and clasps their outstretched, waiting hands, their hazy presence no longer a physical being, but a vibrant energy which swirls and merges somehow within her leading her onto the next path of her journey, not knowing where this will take her.... she steps forward smiling softly, unafraid.

The Box

Jess was leaning back against the café door, closing it against the howling wind when she caught sight of the box behind the counter.

She unwound her scarf from around her neck and took off her coat, hung them up and put her apron on without taking her eyes off the box. She looked questioningly at Jason who shrugged. 'She went about an hour ago and left it under the table. I've brought it back here for safe keeping, I'm sure she will be back in for it later.'

The box belonged to a woman who had started coming into the café about six months ago. 'Bee Woman' was what the staff called her because of the large bumble bee tattoo on her forearm. They had names for most of the customers, not in a disrespectful way, just in a way that helped them identify whose order was whose. There was Cake Hat lady who always wore a crochet hat with a frill round it that was the shape of a sponge cake. And G I Joe who always wore gym clothes and spoke with an American accent and the Pink Panther who was incredibly tall and walked with a slow fluid movement like the pink panther in the cartoon. Jess, a talented artist had filled her sketch book with caricatures of them when things were slow, and Jason said she should sell them, but Jess didn't think they were good enough and didn't want to hurt anyone's feelings.

Lots of customers came through the café, all of them interesting in their own way, but it was 'Bee Woman' who had captured Jess's attention. She came into the café at least three times a week, and always sat in the table by the window. Jess had joked with Jason that she must have hung around outside until that table came free, as she never sat anywhere else. She was medium height and build, with thick black hair shaved up one side. She wasn't the sort of person whose looks made her stand out in a crowd until she fixed her large brown eyes on you. Jess felt like those eyes could see into her very soul, like they were reading her thoughts, shuffling through her mind like you would search through an address book or a dictionary. She felt that her hopes and dreams, her doubts and insecurities were all laid bare to those deep searching eyes and that she was being summed up and judged.

'Bee Woman' always met someone different, usually young women who she spoke to in a low urgent tone, and they leant forward drinking in what she had to say along with their coffees. Occasionally it would be a man in his twenties, those meetings were less urgent and always shorter. Jason had tried listening in a few times, lingering over clearing nearby tables but never managed to pick up anything useful.

But it was the box that was the main talking point. It was about 24 inches by 12 and made of wood. It was more of a small wooden case really as it had a brown leather handle and a brass clasp that was secured by a small brass padlock. Bee Woman was never without it. She would place it on the windowsill, her body blocking it from being touched by anyone but herself. She never opened it to put anything in or take anything out and the odd time she went to the ladies, the box went with her. On one occasion when she spilled her coffee Jess went over to wipe it up. Seeing some had splashed onto the box, she reached out to clean it, but Bee Woman snatched it up and set it on the floor between her black biker style boots.

Jess and Jason spent a lot of the quieter times in the café wondering who Bee Woman really was and what could be in the box. Spy was their favourite choice. They would conjure up scenarios where she was recruiting young women to carry out honey traps on foreign diplomats or engaging them to do undercover work for MI6. Sometimes they would try and guess whether she herself was an undercover police officer helping young women escape pimps or controlling husbands. Mostly though they wondered what was in the box. Jason thought it was one of those radio sets that they had in World War Two, and that she would open it up late at night and tap out a coded message to comrades back in Russia, but he could never come up with what sort of intelligence she could gather in the Copper Kettle café in Lytham that would interest her comrades. Jess thought it could be a wig and some silicone pieces to change her facial features but then decided the box was a little too small.

Jess had done a few sketches of Bee Woman, always from memory. If she really was a spy she didn't want to be caught drawing her. Not that she thought anyone would recognise her from her drawing. Jess's huge talent for art was matched only by her self-doubt. Her application for Art College had sat, unsent, on her laptop for months. The café was safe and easy, there were no challenges or surprises until today when the box had been left behind.

Bee Woman didn't come back for the box that day, or the next. She didn't come the week after that or the next month. Jess had tried to open the padlock, but she didn't try very hard as she wasn't sure she wanted to know what was inside.

The box got pushed further and further back on the shelf until one day Jason decided to have a spring clean. He emptied everything off the shelf, passing items to Jess to swill through a sink of hot soapy water. Finally, he dragged the box out. They both stared at it, they hadn't mentioned Bee Woman for weeks and this reminder piqued their curiosity again. 'Sod it' said Jason, 'I'm opening it.'

He got a pair of pliers from the toolbox in the storeroom and worked on the padlock until it came free. They stood in silence for a few minutes, staring at the clasp and then Jason opened the lid. The box was empty except for a thick cream envelope addressed to Jess. Confused, Jess slid a piece of thick cream notepaper from the envelope covered in a spidery scrawl.

'Dear Jess, I know you have often wondered what was in my box and I am afraid I can't tell you. As I no longer need it, I would like you to have it. Use it for whatever you want, pack your hopes and dreams into it, or maybe your sandwiches for work, whatever you prefer. Personally, I think it's a great box for keeping a sketch pad and some pencils safe. Good luck'

The letter was signed simply with a picture of a bumble bee.

Six months later Jess left college one lunchtime with some friends. She had finally sent off her application along with a portfolio and couldn't believe it when she was accepted into a prestigious art college on the West coast of Scotland. They chattered their way down to the local town for some lunch at their favourite pub. As she waited to cross the road something caught Jess's eye in the window of the little café on the high street. She caught her breath as she took in the sight of Bee Woman sitting at a table in earnest conversation with a young woman. There on the table sat a box, the same as the one Jess now used to carry her sketching materials to class. Behind the counter of the café was another young girl. Jess recognised the curiosity on the girl's face and smiled to herself as she ran to catch up with her friends and enjoy the life Bee Woman had inspired her to grasp.

Rosie

As she packed up her case, Rosie remembered when she first arrived at Dan and Maria's. It felt like a long time ago. She didn't know how long but the seasons had changed more than once and today as she looked out at the frost covering many of the neighbours' cars, Rosie knew that it would nearly be Christmas. There were lights and decorations in the street, and she and Dan had decorated the Christmas tree in the lounge the other day. Dan had told her to make a wish as Christmas was a magical time when wishes would come true. She glanced up at the lady with the kind face and the spotty jumper, Rosie liked her. Her eyes crinkled as she smiled, and she always smelt of strawberries. After she'd left Mummy's house, she'd learnt that it was easier to just hold their hand and trust where they were taking her.

The first home had been horrible. It smelt of cats and she had to sleep on a top bunk which made her feel scared. An older girl called Angela slept below her who often spoke on her phone and told Rosie that the foster carers were mean and would lock her in the cellar if she didn't do what she was told. Rosie was terrified. So terrified that she would often wet the bed which made Angela angry and shouty and the foster mum, Cheryl really annoyed. So annoyed that one day she had to pack her case again and move to another house. Rosie was glad to get away from them.

The second place had a lot of children living there and it was loud and chaotic. But there was a lot of laughter as well as shouting and she liked it. Her foster mum, Diana was really kind, much older than her own Mummy and she had a big squishy tummy and would let Rosie cuddle up and sit there without saying anything. Then one day Diana went to hospital and all the children had to find new homes. That was when she arrived at Dan and Maria's. She liked Dan – he would tell her funny jokes and do colouring with her at the table. But Maria was mean and would often come into her room at night and touch Rosie's things. Rosie would always pretend to be asleep and sometimes Maria would take her covers off her. One night, Maria tried to take the photo of Mummy which Rosie slept with, and Rosie hit her. This made Maria really cross, and she slapped Rosie across the face and told her that she was evil and if she ever did that again, she would never see her Mummy again. Rosie cried herself to sleep most nights.

Maybe that was why she was leaving today – maybe Maria had told the lady with the kind face and spotty jumper how bad she was and so she needed to find her a new home.

Rosie missed Mummy. She remembered dancing in the kitchen in their flat together. Mummy gave the best kisses. But Mummy often fell asleep on the sofa and Rosie would put a cover on her and had to eat biscuits for tea and put herself to bed. She missed her friends at school even though she didn't go very much as Mummy was often asleep in the morning and she wasn't allowed to cross the road by herself. Rosie didn't mind though; she would help Mummy feel better in the mornings by being quiet and bringing her drinks of orange juice or water if there wasn't any juice.

Then one day, she had been off school for a while and the lady with the kind face and spotty jumper came and told Rosie that Mummy wasn't well and needed help and whilst she was getting help, Rosie would have to go and stay somewhere else.

The lady took her hand and gave her a bag with a flower on it and told her to pack her most precious things. Then, she kissed her sleeping Mummy and told her to get better soon. When Rosie had been at Cheryl's for a few days, she found a bottle that smelt like Mummy and hid it in her special bag. It was a green glass bottle, and she would sniff it to bring memories back. She kept that bottle until she got to Dan and Maria's and Maria found It and took it away, saying that she was 'too young and no wonder she was in care' Rosie hadn't understood.

As she got into the silver car - which was clean and shiny inside apart from a few crisps on the floor, she wondered where she would be going to next. Rosie hugged Mr Snuggles tighter – one of her very few links with her home. As they drove in the car, the lady with the kind face and the spotty jumper (whose name was Katie) asked Rosie if she was ready for her surprise. Rosie didn't know much about good surprises so she recoiled at first but the look on Katie's face, was so trusting, she thought perhaps it might be some sweets or a new toy. But why had she had to say goodbye to Dan and Maria.

They drove for a while. About five songs because Rosie counted. Katie always played happy music and Rosie liked it. It was dark outside, and she clutched Mr Snuggles tighter as Rosie had always feared the dark.

As they got out of the car, the cold air hit Rosie's face like a slap from Maria, she buried her head in her coat and stopped looking, trusting the footsteps of Katie to lead her to safety and warmth. She recognised the building as they entered. The lift wasn't working as always and so they had to walk the three flights upstairs to the flat.

Mummy opened the door before they even had a chance to knock and scooped Rosie in her arms. She felt safe again. Mummy smelt different. Mummy looked different, happier. The flat was warm, and the smell of cooking wafted through the hallway. Rosie was scared to let go and she felt tears well up in her eyes.

They sat and snuggled on the sofa whilst Katie put the kettle on, Mummy stroking her face and asking her all sorts of questions. Rosie just smiled and closed her eyes enjoying being back in her Mummy's arms.

'Can I stay for a bit longer?' Rosie asked,

'Yes', said Mummy, 'How about forever?' and Katie smiled.

Rosie thought back to when she made a wish at the Christmas tree with Dan. She'd wished that she could be back home with Mummy.

Dan was right, maybe wishes do come true after all.

An Education

I met Anna at an Open University seminar for first year Humanities students, taking the Introduction to Literature Module. We were both keen to broaden our educational and cultural horizons, beyond 'O' Level and vocational training. She had moved from a small country town, Toombridge, to Belfast, where she trained as a theatre nurse at The City Hospital. She missed her family and was adjusting to city life. I'd recently completed my engineering apprenticeship and was Belfast born and bred.

Like kids set free in a sweet shop, we crammed in everything in front of us: poetry, drama, prose, we couldn't get enough. We were the youngest and I was certainly the loudest in the seminar group. The other members were nice enough people, but more sedate: Malone Road matrons and retired professionals with time on their hands. Looking back, I see how tolerant they were of my animated outbursts and opinionated views. The tutor euphemistically referred to me as, 'energetic', and 'enthusiastic'.

Anna and I often continued our discussions into the coffee-break. I was inclined to be somewhat monochrome in my reading of texts, she would take a more nuanced view, acknowledging that a reading had to allow for some degree of layering and shading.

We were both enthralled with the American novel. The course had F. Scott Fitzgerald's, 'The Great Gatsby', and Ernest Hemmingway's, 'Across the River and Into the Trees', as set books. When the film adaptation of, 'Gatsby', starring Mia Farrow and Robert Redford was released, I had an opportunity to take our relationship beyond the seminar and coffee-break stage. I asked Anna if she fancied going with me to see the movie, quickly adding that it was sure to give us some fresh perspectives on the book, which might be useful for our important forthcoming Tutor Marked Assessments. She readily agreed.

We had a drink afterwards and enthused about the film: the luscious cinematography, how the script perfectly portrayed the decadence of the period and the tragic plight that befell the 'Lost

Generation'. The kind of things you say on a first date, to impress.

I soon moved onto Fitzgerald the writer, conceding that he had an elegant if slightly faded style, fair characterisation and walked you nicely into his convoluted plots. However, not a patch on Hemmingway, the pared back prose, that strips down to the bone.

Getting to the essence of a character in a few sparse sentences, head and shoulders above F. Scott Fitzgerald. Anna began in her usual measured manner. She appreciated Hemingway's terse style, and it had merit. However, Nick Carraway's reflections on the beauty and potential of early America, as he travels Westward by train, sheer poetry: it is wonderful writing.

'Na Anna, with Hemingway you get the real deal, the thingness of things. None of that Fitzgerald stage-setting, posturing crap.'

'Think you're missing the point Martin, we're not talking rugby here, scoring off a scrum, winning tries! Literature's not a competition.'

'Get a grip Anna, it's the best reflection of life, an that's Hemingway.'

'Don't you dare speak that way to me, I've had a bucket full of literature according to Martin Stewart, in the seminars and now on an evening out. Here, I'm away home!'

She was up and through the door. I hurried after her. The stop was near the pub, and an Ormeau Road bus had pulled in and before I could get a word out, doors hissed open, Anna leapt aboard, they hissed closed, and she was gone.

Anna did not attend the next seminar, without her presence the atmosphere felt flat.

'There are some events which must be experienced first-hand, and no amount of recounting or description can match the actuality.... what is Hemingway suggesting here?'

The tutor droned on, I let the others unpick his questions. What an idiot boy, letting a pair of dead American writers cause a rift between me and a very much alive woman.

I dialled her number. Joan, Anna's housemate told me she was working late and would not be home until after eight. She was going out but would make sure Anna got my message.

Walking up the Ormeau Road, a dreary throughfare that meandered from the city centre to the suburbs, I awkwardly carried a bedraggled bunch of white chrysanthemums, bought from a flower-seller at the City Hall, just before she shut the stall. When I passed the Victorian gasworks, it's great gasometers were inhaling noxious coal-gas, that would be pumped into pipes, snaking under the city streets. As I turned on to The Lagan Embankment, I heard a rustling noise on the grassy bank that stretched towards the river, a plump grey rat scurried to the bank's edge and plopped into the turgid water.

I walked to the opposite side of the road and climbed a flight of narrow granite steps, holding tightly an iron rail. There I entered The Holy Land, a red-bricked housing estate, that had been erected by a pious Victorian builder, who on returning from a pilgrimage to the Promised Land, gave the streets in his project Biblical names. I passed through Damascus Street, skirting Jerusalem Street and entering Palestine Street in search of number nine.

At the dark green door, I took a deep breath and lifted the heavy brass knocker, giving it a number of soft, hurried raps. Anna answered, still wearing her nurse's uniform.

'Well, you've a right cheek, Martin Stewart 'thought Joan was slegging me, couldn't see you traipsing over here, after the other night.'

'A peace offering Anna, I was such an eejit after the pictures. Don't know what gets into me. I'm really sorry.'

I pressed the flagging white flowers on her. She took them reluctantly and held them down at her side.

'Don't think you can soft-soap me with your bunch of half dead flowers an' oh Anna I'm so very sorry line. You upset me a lot!'

'Anna I'm dyin' about ya, I'd never ......'

'Give over, do you want the whole street knowing our business, you can come in for a minute, a minute mind you!'

She put the flowers in a green vase of water that stood in the centre of a large table, close to a bottle of red wine.

'I could really do without this now, I've been on my feet all day, had a poor man in theatre for over seven hours, bullet lodged near his heart. Awful business, they just walked into the shop, and his wife and son there'.

'Jesus Anna, I don't know how you deal with that day an' daily. My ma tells me I've not been the same since I saw that wee boy Maguire shot with a rubber bullet an' then helped to lift him off the road, to wait for the ambulance. He died three days later in the children's wing of your place.'

'I remember him, we were all in tears, poor wee lad, he was only seven years of age. You've never mentioned that.'

We sat down at the table, water had plumped up the flowers in the green vase, Anna had her much delayed meal and we shared the wine and our experiences of living in the troubles. The awful toll it took on ordinary people trying to get on with their lives.

The conversation turned to the approaching OU Summer School at Stirling University and how great it would be having a week entirely devoted to course work and other activities, like proper students. We agreed that a break away in Scotland would be very good for both of us.

The Viewing

'I wonder if there is something about the house that made them move?' asked Matt. Their minds full of excitement and wonder after meeting Kathy and looking around what they hoped would be their new home.

Shore House had been vacant for a long time, but as soon as Jessie and Matt spotted it online, they knew it was the house for them. Within their budget and in the catchment area for the best primary and secondary schools (should the time come to expand their family). They weren't afraid of hard work and presumed it would be 'a bit of a project' which is what they wanted. A house to grow with them over the years.

Jessie had just been promoted at Sunrise Bank and Matt's graphic design business was really beginning to take off. As he was able to work from home it meant the promotion for Jessie and the move had been easy to accept.

Settle View was the perfect destination. A small coastal town with a parade of shops on the seafront that sold bespoke jewellery and inexpensive designer clothes interspersed with high end independent coffee shops and unique looking restaurants. Its easy commute to the more aspirational nearby town which attracted young artistic couples like Jessie and Matt who were looking for that next stage in their lives.

Jessie and Matt impulsively decided to drive over there on the Sunday, just to have a look at the house from the outside, after viewing it online the night before. Just to see what the neighbourhood was like and get a general feel for the house. They exchanged conspiratorial smiles, excited at the future that lay ahead of them.

Shore House was positioned at the end of a cul-de-sac, and stood somewhat imposing, twice the size of most of the other houses. The outside of the house was truly breath-taking. A beautiful Georgian style detached house. Its symmetrically placed windows seeming to follow their gaze as they gaped unbelievingly at the building in front of them. The photos they had seen the night before had not done it justice.

Jessie's heart skipped a beat.

'It's beautiful' she whispered to Matt who was staring open-mouthed.

'Let's have a look around' said Matt, excited.

It clearly needed some tidying up on the outside. The garden was covered in enormous weeds which also crept up the side of the house. As they made their way towards the front door, they stepped through the overgrown foliage, hiding the once neat pathway. It was as if somehow the garden was beginning to wrap around the house in a protective manner almost preventing anyone getting to the front door.

They peaked through one of the windows, but it was too difficult to see anything due to the amount of dirt and dust. Although it was obvious that the house was empty, as they looked around, it felt impolite not to check in case anyone was there, so they rang the bell.

'You never know' said Jessie, 'An estate agent may be showing someone around.'

'On a Sunday?' sneered Matt, 'No chance!'

To their utter surprise, the door was opened by a woman in her 50s. She had well kept highlighted blond hair cut neatly into a wavy chin length bob. She wore a royal blue twin set, with a pale silk blouse and a chunky blue necklace. She looked like she was dressed up for a special occasion.

'Oh… er… sorry' said Jessie apologetically, 'We were just in the area and we wanted to have a look at the house. We didn't think anyone would be here.'

'Come in, come in' said the lady with a welcoming smile, 'I'm Kathy. I used to live here'.

Kathy was friendly and led them into a hallway that was full of cobwebs reminiscent of an abandoned house. It was strange to see the contrast of the unkemptness of the house and Kathy herself who was incredibly smart for a Sunday morning. She didn't offer any explanation about either the state of the place or why she was there.

Jessie and Matt asked the usual questions asked when viewing a house – what are the schools like? Is the area nice? What are the neighbours like?

When they asked why they moved, Kathy's whole demeanour changed. A wave of sadness filled the air and brushed over her face. Her eyes dropped to the floor.

'It was just our time to move on'.

This discouraged them from probing any further – both wondering if perhaps this family had experienced some tragedy or loss.

The house had that old dusty smell that you sometimes get in a charity shop when things haven't been aired for a while, but besides the obvious need for a clean and some updating, the house was in surprisingly good condition with so much potential.

As they drove away, they both felt an anticipation in their stomachs. Both agreed. Next morning, they would call the estate agent to put in an offer.

As soon as Jessie arrived at work she rang. No answer. They eventually answered on her third attempt, the agent surprised when Jessie said that she wanted to make an offer on Shore House.

'But don't you want to view it first?' she asked.

'Oh well…we saw it yesterday. We swung by on a whim and the owner just happened to be there and showed us around'.

A long silence on the phone.

'But that's impossible' said the estate agent, 'That house has been empty for years.'

Suddenly Jessie felt a bit uneasy. Something was not quite right. Meanwhile her phone pinged – a message from Matt which just read OPEN and there was a newspaper article attached.

'I guess the owners still have a key then?' questioned Jessie, distracted as she tried to open Matt's message.

'Err, that's actually not possible' hesitated the estate agent. 'The previous owners are er… no longer around'.

Jessie's blood ran cold.

'So, who was it who was showing us around then? Who was Kathy?'

She glanced at her phone as Matt's message appeared. An old newspaper article, the headline…

'*Family of 5 murdered in quaint suburban coastal town*'.
And there in the middle of a family photo was Kathy, smiling, wearing the exact same outfit they had seen her in the day before.

The Bookshop

Sarah sat on the bench in the watery sunshine, let her gaze wander over the Village Bookshop across the road and allowed herself to be transported back fifty years.

Although the village had changed over the years and had grown into a small town, the bookshop was exactly as it was when she first went through the red front door as a six-year-old child.

Corbishley was a small village back in the seventies. There were the usual shops down the narrow main street. 'Bowers the bakers' enticed people in with the smell of freshly baked bread and a display of cakes in the window that Sarah and her best friend Bess drooled over every Saturday morning. They skipped past Stanleys, the fish shop as fast as they could, turning their faces away from the dead eyes of the fish lying in their icy graves. There was 'Cassidy's', the greengrocers with colourful fruit and veg stacked outside on wooden barrels and then 'Tears Butchers' with its sawdust floor and brown greaseproof paper for wrapping the various cuts of meat.

The 'Village bookshop' was the grandest building on the main street. It was a narrow building, three storeys high. The front was painted white and wore black beams across the upper two floors with pride. The bay window on the ground floor was well lit with spotlights and fairy lights around the frame. The large, deep windowsill carried an ever-changing display of the latest books aimed at enticing in budding chefs, blood thirsty crime readers or avid gardeners depending on the current releases. You entered the shop through a red door with a brass latch and a brass bell inside tinkled to let the shopkeeper know you had arrived.

Inside the shop were floor to ceiling mahogany bookshelves arranged in order of subject or in the case of fiction, in alphabetical order of the author's name. A few coffee tables were dotted around surrounded by fraying, well-worn red wing back chairs that invited shoppers to sit for a while and browse the books. The smell of wood polish and paper was mixed with the scent of candlewax from the candlelight readings that the owner held once a month. At the rear of the shop was a step down into the children's section. The bookshelves here were lower and brightly coloured rugs were scattered on the worn carpet. Colourful posters advertising the latest exciting adventures of the secret seven or the current fantastical nonsense conjured up by Dr Seuss and Roald Dahl were dotted around the walls and some low tables had crayons and pictures for small children to colour while their older siblings chose a book.

It was this part of the shop that Sarah and Bess went to every Saturday morning while their mothers did some shopping. Sarah's mum had seen the poster for story time stuck in the front window and had put the girls' names down. They weren't too keen when they were told, they were both a little bit scared of the lady who owned the shop. Mrs Owen was a tall lady with long jet-black hair tied up in a colourful scarf. Her clothes were long and flowing and her dark eye makeup made her seem exotic to the small girls. They didn't have the words then, but now they would describe her as a bit hippyish.

She lived upstairs on the top floor of the shop and would clatter down the wooden stairs with a book under her arm and a mug of a steamy minty smelling drink, not like the ordinary tea their mothers drank by the bucket load.

She always had a small cloth bag across her body that held a notebook curled at the edges and a gold pen with a tassel on. Sarah and Bess called this her word collecting book. Mrs Owen always had radio four playing in the background and if she wasn't dealing with a customer, she was heard muttering to herself about interesting words or phrases she had heard that would then be written in her book. The girls wondered what she did with those words. Were they prisoners in the upstairs flat? Sarah thought she must have drawers stuffed full of them, and when she wanted to write something she would open a drawer and they would all fight to be set free and chosen to be weaved into a story. Bess thought she kept them in teapots and poured herself drinks of words when she ran out.

Mrs Owen would read a different story each week and then give the children a piece of paper and a pencil so they could draw something from the story or write their own version of it. She always encouraged them to think of different endings and Sarah and Bess would giggle together and think of the most ridiculous endings that would shock Mrs Owen.

Sarah's favourite topic was about an old lady who had found the secret of how to live forever. Mrs Owen was always most interested in Sarah's writing and would often call Mr Owen down to the shop to read her latest offering. Mr Owen was a tall thin man who dressed entirely in black. He had a row of yellow teeth that reminded Sarah of the ivory keys on her grandmother's decrepit piano. Whenever Mr Owen came into the shop Sarah would feel a chill and would shiver when he inevitably patted her on the head with his long bony fingers.

The girls went to story time for about a year until the lure of dance classes and sleepovers with friends took over and they happily abandoned the bookshop and their fantasies about Mrs Owen's prison for words in her flat upstairs.

Sarah shook her head and brought herself back to the present. Fifty years had passed and Corbishley had grown into a small town. Outcrops of new boxy housing estates had sprung up. Young couples with two point four children moved in and the old traditional shops had made way for coffee shops and beauty salons.

Sarah, now a published author of a series of fantasy books had been amazed to see the bookshop was still there. She crossed the road and there in the centre of the window was a display of her books based around the woman who had found the secret to eternal life. She pushed open the door and the same brass bell tinkled her arrival. Radio four was playing in the background and the woman behind the counter looked up. Sarah gasped in shock, her mind racing. It had definitely been fifty years since she had been here but here was Mrs Owen looking exactly the same as she had then. It couldn't be possible. 'Hello Sarah' she said. 'I always knew you would be back just as I always knew you would be a writer. Come on upstairs, you look a little pale. I will put the kettle on and brew you up a nice cup of words.'

Caught in a Trap

Joe woke up in a cold sweat.

He was back in his old bedroom at home, half asleep. He could hear the familiar sounds of the door slamming and the shouting begin, his mother screaming at his dad. The sound of things being thrown, and after a few minutes, silence, before his dad's heavy steps, trudging up the stairs, the opening and closing of the spare bedroom door and then nothing.

Along with the cold, clammy sweat, he felt a sense of despair, as though things would never get better. The feeling that he was on a treadmill from which there was no escape. Now at least he could jump into the shower, and let the hot water wash away his nightmares.

Joe had never shared these nightmares with anyone. He would just tell himself to relax, to pull himself together, and they would disappear. They did, for a while, but it was almost as though subconsciously he was willing them back, because they would always return, and with them the same unanswered questions.

Why did Mother and Dad row so much? Was it something he did, or said that triggered their nightly rows? Why did neither parent ever open up and share things?

It was the morning of his Mother's Funeral. Joe was home on compassionate leave from the Army, his life since joining as a young man of eighteen.

As he dressed, he recalled the first time he came home in his Army fatigues, after three months training at Catterick Army camp. He had left home a rather overweight, unfit teenager, but now returned as a fitter, healthier and confident young man.

His dad was very proud of him and showed it.

'Come here Joe' he smiled and gave him a bear hug which Joe returned.

'What have the Army done to my Joe!' He exclaimed laughing.

'I'm just the same Joe' Joe replied smiling.

'Just a bit fitter and healthier' he added.

'Mother, come and see the new Joe.' His dad went on.

He recalled vividly that Mother had shown little interest, giving him just an almost friendly peck on the cheek.

'Hello Joe' she muttered as she briefly held him, before backing away.

His mother's cool attitude had made him wonder ......she had been against him joining the Army, but the atmosphere at home was so toxic, that he had to go, and persuaded his dad to give his approval.

To the outside world, their family must have seemed quite normal. Dad went off to work every morning at eight o'clock sharp, cycling into the local town for his job as a Clerk in the local Gas Works. He came home at the same time every night, had supper with his family, and then disappeared to the pub till closing time. This was normal for a working man back in the sixties, the pub being a refuge from the pressures of work and the demands of family.

He did this every night of the week except Sunday nights, and the strange thing was that Joe could never remember him suffering from a hangover the next day. He guessed that some people just had that unique ability to drink without it affecting them.

40

As the rows happened when Dad came home, Joe assumed that they were related to what happened at the pub. Mother never shared her feelings, so he was none the wiser.

Looking back, Joe could not remember too much about his grandparents or any other family member, except his Auntie Sheila, his mother's sister. Auntie Sheila was the one person he could confide in, although even she became tight lipped when asked about their life growing up as sisters.

He got the feeling that it was a closed door, a door that Auntie Sheila would rather remain shut, only volunteering that the family was 'dysfunctional' as she put it.

She was a spinster, a few years older than Mother, and lived alone in the house they had both grown up in. Their parents, his grandparents, had both long since died, and with Mother in a home of her own, it made sense that Auntie Sheila inherited the house. Mother always gave the impression that she wanted nothing to do with the old family home, in fact Joe could not remember a time when they ever visited Auntie Sheila. When they did meet, it was always at their house and only on special occasions like Christmas.

While Joe had a good relationship with his dad, he would say little about the nightly rows. His dad simply dismissing them as normal husband and wife rows, nothing to worry about. Joe sensed there was more to it, but in the absence of any willingness from his dad to say any more, he remained in ignorance.

The next few years of Joe's life in the Army were a revelation. He discovered that the Army was a large family in which everyone looked out for each other. He discovered a natural ability to lead, and had to admit to himself if no one else, that he didn't miss his home life.

On his last visit home, he realised that Mother was not well.

Her memory was fading, and she was struggling to do even the simple things. Dad was also a shadow of his former self, clearly worried about her.

Joe asked Auntie Sheila to help, and thankfully she moved in to take care of Mother while Dad was at work, and make sure she was safe.

When Joe's leave came to an end, he was grateful to have Auntie Sheila to take care of the home and Mother.

On his last night, after Mother went to bed, and Dad was out, Sheila opened up to Joe, and talked about her childhood.

The girls had grown up in a loveless family, with a father who not only beat their mother, but also used to slap the girls for any minor transgression. They both grew up thinking that violence was a natural part of family life.

Joe wondered to himself as he lay in bed that night, why would Mother marry a man like her dad after all the trauma of her childhood?

He felt anger at his dad for what he now thought was his systematic abuse of Mother, and yet pity at this pathetic old man who was now doing his best to look after his wife when she needed him.

It was not long after his return from leave that he received the news of his dad's sudden death.

Joe received the news with a sense of relief as well as sadness. He was after all his dad for all his faults, while at the same time Joe could not forget the way he had treated his wife, Joe's mother, all those years.

It was after the funeral, which was sparsely attended, that Auntie Sheila said she had something to tell Joe.

She told Joe that shortly before Dad's death, they were talking about Mother's failing health, and Dad told her that Mother had been abusing him for years. She had confided in him just after they got married about her dad's abuse, and he promised to protect her as long as they both lived.

It was mental abuse, although things were also regularly thrown at him, when he came back from the pub. He freely admitted that he went to the pub every night, partly to escape from the abuse, but also because he worked behind the bar every night bar Sunday to save money for Joe. He then showed Sheila his will and asked her to be his Executor. He made her promise not to tell Joe until after his death.

Joe was completely thrown by this news; he found it hard to comprehend or believe, but as he went over everything in his mind, things started to fit into place, Dad's need to get out of the house whenever he could, his reluctance to open up to what was really going on.

Sheila paused and told him, 'Your Dad loved your mother despite everything, and the one stipulation was that you should never blame her and take care of her until she passes '.

She added 'you will see in the will that he has left £25,000 to you, the proceeds of working long hours in the pub all those years. He hoped that it would in some way make up for your unhappy childhood and give you and maybe your own family one day, a better life.

His admiration for his dad never ended, he had remained true to his marriage vows to love honour and cherish and had done his best to protect his son from the horror of his mother's behaviour throughout his life.

All that remained now was to give her the Funeral she would have wanted and for Joe to forgive her and tell her he loved her. A sad story of two lives damaged by one man.

Saving Grace

Lost in his own thoughts, he didn't notice her at first. Thoughts that now, on reflection seemed futile and unnecessary. But when he had, he realised that unless he acted, nothing would ever be the same for him again. So, he raced towards her.

Joel Green was twenty-five. He had just secured his first 'proper job' as a Marketing Assistant in a Start Up company in Manchester. He loved the city - the buzz, the people, the life, and the culture, and having spent longer than most as a student here, he was loving life even more now that he had a bit more money to enjoy it with.

The early evening air was grey and damp, with a mist that hovered awkwardly over the bridge making it difficult to see detail. The dazzling headlights below suggested impatient drivers seemingly unaware of and disinterested in the events taking place so close.

Joel had climbed over the railings of the bridge by Deansgate station before he had even had a chance to process his own thoughts. Before he could even say to himself 'What the hell am I doing?' he found himself perched on the ledge of the bridge overlooking this cityscape about four feet away from her.

'Go away' she snapped, 'And don't tell me not to do it'.

'I'm not going to. I just want to make sure you do it properly'.

She turned then to face him. Joel smiled awkwardly trying not to show the fear in his own face. Her blue eyes were wide, her whole body shaking. She looked about the same age as Joel and he wondered what had brought her here, sitting on the wrong side of a bridge on a cold Autumn evening in Manchester.

'I'm Joel'

'Grace'

'I would shake your hand, but I kind of need it to hang on in here'.

Although she sniffed at his measly attempt at humour her face softened slightly. He tried to shuffle closer to her, but she panicked and shouted.

'Don't come any closer!'

'I'm not, I was just err…getting comfy'

She raised her eyebrows.

'So, err… Grace. Do you come here often?' She exhaled slowly and closed her eyes for a moment.

'Really?' she groaned.

Joel looked at her innocently, unsure of where this conversation was heading.

'What do you mean?'

'Trying to chat me up, are you?' She snapped.

'Do you want me to?'

'No!'

'What do you want me to do?'

'Leave me alone'

'Mm about that. I'm kind of stuck here now'.

'Well, can't you just climb back up?'

45

'Well, I could if I err....'

'If you what?'

'If I wasn't scared of heights!'

This couldn't help but make Grace snigger.

'Of all the heroes, I get to try and save me, I get someone scared of heights. Bloody typical!'

'Yep, you really lucked out. In fact, I'm feeling a bit lightheaded right now...'

Joel's head began to sway, as he tried to breathe out slowly. The cold damp Manchester air hitting his lungs with a force he wasn't expecting. The mist enveloping the bridge rising casually, creating a cocoon around them. Only them.

It was as if only they existed in this moment. This was all that mattered. Joe momentarily forgot where he was, focusing only on his breathing and the blueness of Grace's eyes.

Grace sensed his panic and, after a moment's hesitation, reluctantly shifted over towards Joel placing her hand tentatively on his shoulder.

'You, OK?'

'Yes, thank you. Now you're here though, can I buy you a drink?'

Grace withdrew and shook her head in disgust.

'Pathetic. You men are all the same.' Her face fell as if this had taken her to some dark place and Joel lost her again, the faraway look in her eyes returning. The faint hiss of the traffic moving slowly over the road below disturbed the misty silence that surrounded them.

'Hey' he said, 'It might not be OK now, but it will be'.

'It won't ever be the same again', she replied.

'It might not be the same as before, but I promise you it will be OK'.

Grace started to cry then, her face full of vulnerability and despair. Joel felt as he was losing her into the mist that was surrounding them. He managed to grab her hand and she turned to face him.

'I don't know what I'm doing' She confessed in barely more than a whisper.

'Me neither.' Joel grimaced, 'But how about we try and work it out together'.

Joel watched the pain and despair in her face shift to fear and disorientation. Like she'd woken up from a dream and didn't know where she was. Her body sagged in defeat.

'I don't want to jump'.

'Me neither' said Joel, placing his other hand up to gently touch her on the shoulder. 'How about we help each other climb back up?'

Joel soon discovered that climbing back up wasn't as easy as climbing down. Fear overtook the adrenalin rush and his feet struggled to grip the muddy banks. He tried to grab the cold and slippery railings but lost his footing and momentarily let go of Grace who stumbled backwards. Before saving himself, Joel shouted out in horror,

'Grace!'

'I'm ok' she reassured him, as she wobbled uncertainly on the ledge.

He was even more terrified that Grace would change her mind and pull back than he was of himself falling. Momentarily forgetting his own fear, he leant out towards her,

'Grab my hand'.

She glanced down and then back up to meet Joel's reassuring face and tentatively held out her hand once again. This time, Joel used all his mental and physical strength to focus on getting them safely over to the right side of the bridge. Unaware of anything else going on around them he clung to Grace, fighting through his own fears to help her climb the twenty or so remaining slippery steps. Nothing else mattered.

Rust from the bridge supports bit into their frozen fingers as they climbed.

'Don't look down'.

'I'm not!'

Finally, they made it over the bridge to safety, bending hands on knees as they fought to gather their breath. As Joel straightened up Grace properly looked at him again – this young, handsome man who didn't know her but who had risked his own life for her.

'I don't know how to thank you.'

'Anytime. Well, I mean – you're not going to do that again are you?'

'No, not today anyway' She smiled reassuringly and walked away. Below, the lights and sounds of the background traffic remained unchanged, the commuters still oblivious to events

happening above them. Joel noticed that the evening mist was
beginning to lift.

'Grace?'

She turned around yet continued to walk backwards.

'Fancy that drink now?'

'I'd love to'.

The Blowin

John walked up the brae towards Lough Annan, taking a shortcut along an old right-of- way that had been in times past used to access remote cottages, now collapsed stone skeletons; a few empty window casings staring vacantly out on the Atlantic. Those who had once belonged there, long dead or evicted, scattered to the four winds.

He was still exploring his new environment, getting to know the lay of the land and making an effort to acquaint himself with his neighbours. It would take time to build another life here. In his darkest moments there was doubt that he ever would. Those nights lying awake listening to the pounding of the Atlantic breakers on the stony shore, the gales tirelessly searching the cottage walls and roof, seeking out a weak spot. Maura's absence, a cold, hard fact, like the stone in the walls and just as unresponsive to his cries and tears. Would he always be reaching into that emptiness, when half asleep he stretched across the bed?

The snorting of a horse broke the morning quiet, a man not much older than John, was standing at a five-bar gate, pouring soy-nuts into a trough bolted to the middle bar. A white mare was eagerly nuzzling and chomping her fodder, a shy grey foal partly hidden behind her left flank. The man's close engagement with the animals caused John to feel like an intruder, and his instinct was to quietly pass-by. The horseman turned to lift a bridle, that lay across a brush and curry comb on the grass and became aware of John.

'Great morning to be out, Daley, John Daley, I'm over at the old Housten place.'

'Seamus Magee, pleased to mak' yer acquaintance'.

'Lovely horses'

'Got the mare af oul' Johnny Housten, she's a goodin, haf Connemara.'

'Fine animal, I can see her in the foal, I'll let you get on, might see you in the Strand for a pint sometime?'

'Indeed, ya might.

He would have to be careful, after Maura's death he was a fixture in The White Horse. Brendan, the landlord, had threatened to charge him rent for his stool at the bar, the closest he could get to telling him his drinking was out of control. Old friends from his days with McAlpine and Wimpy, who like himself had settled in Shepherd's Bush way before the start of its gentrification, were less diplomatic:

'For Jasus sake John, catch yerself on! Get a grip, or everything you and Maura worked so hard for will go down the pan, an' you along with it.'

The Strand Bar was the place where children's heads were wet after Christenings, weddings were celebrated and a drink would be taken, to wish those who had been buried in Maghery cemetery on their way. Con, the landlord provided counselling services, if business was slack.

John ordered a pint of Guinness, and as he waited for the ritual of its pouring and settling to be completed, his eye's adjusted to the dim light of the bar. He noticed Seamus Magee sitting alone at a table beside the turf fire, cradling an empty whiskey glass.

'Hi Seamus, get you a drink, what you on.'

'Large Paddy.'

'Con, when you've done my pint, a large Paddy for Seamus.'

Con put the settling Guinness on the bar and made a horizontal slicing action with his right hand.

'He's had a load already John, an' not in great form'.

'Con, he's a neighbour, and I want to buy him a drink.'

'Fair enough, on your head....'

When the drinks were placed on the table, Seamus Magee lifted his whiskey and emptied the glass. He stared at John Daley, whose presence seemed to remind him of something very important, that he was having difficulty bringing to mind.

'You fecking Blowins, waltzing over here with yer eassy money, buying up everything in front of ya. If our Michael had got half a chance of a house here, he'd have not had to venture anywhere near Birmingham. It broke my Sarah's heart, him dying like that over there. Ya fecking Blowin bastards.'

He lurched at John, knocking him backwards from his chair, then attempting to punch him, but Con and a couple of regulars moved quickly and ushered Seamus towards the door.

'Yur well out of order there Seamus, an yur barred. Danny take him home an try an settle 'im. Sorry about that John, have a Jameson, ya cud do with one after that carry-on, I'm Sure.'

'No thanks all the same Con, I'm gon'a call it a night. See ya '

Leaving the pub, he breathed in the warm, still evening, foxes called on the hill; the intoxicating fragrances of Elderflower and Meadowsweet, came from the fields and hedgerows, enveloping him with a sense of Midsummer promise. Beyond the end of Maghery Strand, a thin ribbon of red-gold waves, showed where the sun had gone down. Arriving at the cottage, John pushed open the unlocked door, closing it quietly.

'Blow-in, don't think so.'

He was roused from deep sleep by loud banging on the front door and the sound of agitated voices and clattering tractor engines. Martin Sweeny, a local farmer was outside.

'John, yid better shift yerself, there's gorse fires all over the place.'

'Near here?'

'Yer safe enough for the minute, who knows what way thill shift? We're heading to Meenacross, 'ti see hire Seamus Magee 's fairin' the fires stalkin' all round his place.'

'I'll grab my coat and boots an give youse a hand.'

Walking towards the tractors hitched to tank-sprayers, and parked Jeeps, he could see dull red fire covered by an umbrella of black smoke in the distance. The gently undulating landscape, between the sea and the mountains, had always seemed a benign place, now in the grip of the raging fires it was a place of destruction: consuming vegetation, wildlife, livestock, and dwellings. Martin, pointed to a white Nissan jeep.

'There's room in that one John. I'll be behind ya's with the spray-tank, we better get shifting to Magee's.'

The jeep moved down the brae, getting closer to the worst of the fires. John could now fully appreciate the danger they posed:

'Jasus! I'd no notion, things were this bad.'

'Bad do ya say, I've bin up half th' night, trying to save a wee holiday cottage over at Ire' place, belonging to English people, but the thatch caught an th' whole place went up. Hope we're in time for Magee's.'

'God, same here.'

As they neared Magee's it became clear the fire was creeping from the burning bog and spreading up the sloping bank at the back of the house, towards the stable. John leapt from the Jeep, ignoring the driver's shouts to wait for a spray-tank and more help. He sprinted up the gravel drive towards the house and stable, small flames were dancing like fairy lights in the lower branches of the trees that sheltered the stable, fire was beginning to scorch the wooden panelling at it's rear. Thirty feet in front of the stable door lay Seamus Magee, his white shirt blackened with soot and smoke, blood oozed from a gash at his temple.

'Jasus, get ma horses out, save them whatever ya' do.'

Grabbing Seamus under the arms he dragged him down the drive towards the temporary safety of the track where vehicles were parked. Laying him gently on the grass verge he turned and ran back towards the endangered stable. One of the rescuers cried out:

'Don't go near, the flames are catching the back!'

John kicked in the stable door and darted to the stall, pulling a couple of halters from a hook on the wall, he spoke softly to the spooked mare and foal as he slipped them over their heads. Smoke and flames were starting to leap above the skirting boards at the backend of the stable, as the fire clawed its way in. He gently ushered the mare and her foal out of the stall and stable towards the brae and the waiting rescue party. A women took the halter ends and lead the horses away. John made his way to Seamus Magee, who was laying on a makeshift stretcher, waiting to be placed on the flat bed of a Toyota pick-up. He grabbed his hand:

'Jasus Seamus, that was a near thing'.

'John, ya got ma horses out, I don't know what I'd a ….you're a good neighbour John an I'm sure we'll be great friends.'

'You concentrate on getting well Seamus, I'll take care of the horses.'

Ten Words

Maureen stared at the piece of paper with the 10 words written on it and sighed. She had been told to write down 10 separate words on the piece of paper and had guessed that they would be asked to write a story using the words. She had also guessed that they would have to swap pieces of paper so she had chosen random words that she wouldn't want for herself. That was where she had gone wrong, they were told to take their own piece of paper and now she was stuck with ten stupid words and no idea what to write.

Maureen had joined the creative writing group a few months earlier hoping it would reignite her passion for words and writing. That was until it all came crashing down and her love affair with words ended abruptly.

She had grown up with a deep love of words in a house filled with books and journals and newspapers.

Her mother was an author and Maureen's earliest memories of her were of a tall woman with messy brown hair, a ready smile, and a battered notebook always to hand. The notebook travelled everywhere with her mother who would stop what she was doing to scribble down a word or a phrase that caught her imagination, or to Maureen's embarrassment, snatches of conversation overheard in the supermarket or coffee shop. It once took an hour and a half to buy some breakfast cereal because Maureen's mum was busy noting down a chat between two women in the bread aisle of Sainsbury's.

Maureen was in awe of her mother's talent and the number of books she had written. She always dreamt of being a famous novelist, tripping over ideas and plot lines in her attic room, messages of congratulations and requests for book signings coming in from her agent. Writing fiction just didn't seem to happen for Maureen though. Instead, she followed her father into journalism, writing fact suited her better and she wrote for a local paper.

She moved up through the ranks and became a lead writer for a popular woman's magazine, doing interview pieces with minor celebrities and some lifestyle articles. She had just started adding content to the magazines social media account when disaster struck, and a complaint hit the editor's desk that Maureen had 'misgendered' a local rap artist. The editor had to explain carefully to Maureen what the problem was and despite promising it wouldn't happen again Maureen was a little confused. A few months later two more complaints came in accusing Maureen of ageism and racism. Maureen was horrified.

She had run a piece about MAMILS (middle aged men in Lycra) and commented on the effect the cycling group had on the Women's Institute afternoon tea party. She managed to offend the good ladies of the WI who argued there was no age limit on ogling men in tight clothing, and the MAMILS themselves who argued that there was no age limit on wearing Lycra and it wasn't their fault if they set hearts fluttering in the tea shop.

She had also written a piece on the rise of the onesie as the chosen method of clothing for students and questioned whether a Burka onesie would be a popular item for students in Leeds. While Maureen had thought this was a brilliant idea, she heard words such as racist, stereotyping and a few others she simply didn't understand.

These incidents led to dismissal, confusion and a decree absolute between Maureen and Words. She found herself in new territory where words weren't just words any more, they were things to be taken, twisted, and used against people to promote whatever ideology a particular group had at any given time. They were taken by politicians and put through a process to make even the most shocking situation seem palatable to the masses. They were used to spread guilt and fear. They were used to promote hate and turn the things Maureen thought she knew on their heads. It was a minefield she couldn't cope with, and she walked away from writing and threw herself into running a charity shop instead.

Maureen missed writing and that was why, after a couple of years away from the love of her life she forced herself to join the writing group. And now here she was staring at these ten words and trying to come up with a story. Old wounds ran deep though and caused endless anxiety. There was a kettle, but what happened if the pot called the kettle black? She could put the lamp on the table and turn it on, but would that offend someone who had sight problems? And if she turned the lamp off, would they fall over the shoes and sue her? What if the plant was a weed? Would it be a garden weed or cannabis weed? That could get her in more trouble. Could she use the phone to google a story? Maybe the binary calculator wanted to be identified as non-binary? Should she pull the rug out from under this whole ridiculous tale and use the pen to start a different story?

In the end Maureen packed her ten words into the rucksack and decided she was still out of love with words and would join a gardening club instead.

Maureen's ten words

Kettle
Lamp
Plant
Rucksack
Shoes
Table
Rug
Pen
Phone
Binary Calculator

The Sands of Time

Dave frowned, a trait he was known to frequently exhibit, his face taking on a look that his wife said he 'couldn't erase'. He didn't understand exactly what she meant by that, but she said it often enough, too often in fact. Not knowing whether it was a compliment or not he hadn't dared to ask.

This time Dave's frown resulted from him recently recalling the words of a song that he used to sing at school at Christmas time, every Christmas in fact, for years. School days that were many years ago when Christmas songs had to be learned off by heart and were bound never to leave your mind. They were designed to dip in and out of your memory, for life, sometimes disappearing for years but never failing to return.

As a child you didn't know this would happen, but it did. It wasn't a purposeful or minded recall but one of those moments where the words arrived on their own, uninvited and unannounced, infiltrating mind and memory.

For Dave however it was the first time he had thought of this particular song since those old school days and the words returned with a vengeance. '*The Sands of Time Run Slow*'. He stroked his balding head and frowned again. The sun was shining outside, and he was annoyed with the words in his head – it wasn't Christmas after all.

Dave felt unusually uneasy and unsettled. He was known to his friends as a cheerful chap with a warm character, physically tall, when he managed to stand up straight, and, he liked to think, good looking or as, he was known to say, debonair. His current mood was out of character.

He had been successful at work and had reached the top management level of the company he had happily worked for. He had earned his own office with his name on the door, a decent salary, a building full of enthusiastic staff and, typical those days, an attentive secretary.

He had the luxury of a good pension, or a 'full pension' as his financial adviser reminded him, to which Dave always quipped, in quick response, had been 'bloody well earned'.

Now old age had arrived, and he no longer felt in control of everything. He was waiting for his knee to be repaired. It was, he had been told, 'complicated', Dave was not comfortable with complications; they just didn't happen.

He looked round his small, crowded room deep in thought. He stared at a stack of neatly piled papers on the antique desk, several pens arranged in order and glanced at the corner of the room where, sat beside the double-glazed window, framed by a number of small panes of glass, were his beloved golf clubs.

The clubs had been carefully placed there with the woods lovingly wrapped in their branded golf head covers. Dave made sure that the young, over enthusiastic cleaner who called in weekly had been issued with clear instructions not to go anywhere near them.

The window overlooked the rear garden, the lawn cut beautifully, manicured, and mown to a particularly low level in places, so that Dave could practice his putting.

At the far end of the lawn was a metal putting cup sunk into the grass. It was marked by a large, red flag for Dave to perfect his chipping. The flag was flapping from right to left in the blustery wind and Dave eyed the number '4' clearly marked on it, in white dye and glistening in the spring sunshine. It stood proudly over the grass, which was longer than usual, as Dave had not been out practicing his swing for a while.

'The Sands of Time Run Slow' – there it was again, those words, that lyric, that ancient lyric.

Dave stood up slowly and reached for his oversized crimson jumper, pulling it on over his head. The jumper was comforting and warm, made of a soft wool blend and he tugged it down over his waist with ease. It was fondly known as his 'Pop' jumper, as he had been told quite seriously, by his friend's ten-year-old grandson, that it made him look like his favourite grandad but, as he had a range of similar jumpers in all the colours of the rainbow, he didn't know why this one had been picked out. The thought made him smile and his cragged, weather-beaten face lightened a little.

The lyrics reminded Dave that the sands of time did indeed run slow but, like Christmas, things always come in their own time. Dave knew this was true, but he was impatient. Making sure that things happened when they needed to had been his job, his life.

'When, when…?' He must have muttered that word, those words out loud.

'Oh, Lovie.' said a quiet voice from outside the room and his wife's face appeared by the door 'it will happen. You'll be sorted soon, I'm sure'.

'Huh!' retorted Dave shrugging his shoulders to accentuate his unhappiness. He knew he would have to wait, accept what he was told and hope everything would be just right.

And so, time passed by, and he felt a continuing sadness having to delay his well-made plans – a holiday, games of golf, walking days with the rambling club.

Until he received the phone call he had been waiting for.

Now the feeling was different, a feeling of warm relief which he enjoyed. Time had passed. Spring had turned into summer and summer had stretched to winter. Recalling his thoughts from the start of the year Dave smiled, simply content that he had survived and was recovering. He was at last on his long-awaited holiday.

He cheerfully looked around, at the blue sky, the choppy sea, and the glistening sand. He reached out in front of him and bent to touch the warm, golden-brown grains, picked up a handful and admired them, allowing them to slowly disappear through his fingers. He smiled and teasingly frowned at his wife. 'Never erase that look' she reminded him in a fond whisper and his frown turned into a smile as he kissed her.

The sands of time had taken on a new meaning as had that frown. He had waited for this moment for so long, it felt. It was easy now to laugh, looking back. His friends had teased him that, after all, he had only needed a half knee repair and not what they called 'a complicated full one'.

As he phoned to confirm his tee time at the Mauritius Golf Club, those lyrics came into his head from nowhere as he closed off the call - the sands of time can run as slowly as they like now, he thought contentedly, smiling at the bag of golf clubs by the door.

Rowan

Ann was a serial killer – of house plants. She killed them with kindness, overwatering and overfeeding, lavishing loving attention on them until nothing was left but a stick in a pot. The latest victim was a winter cactus, a present from her son, a tangible expression of the triumph of hope over experience. It arrived with glossy green leaves and creamy white buds destined never to fulfil their promise and bloom. John christened his wife's attempts at indoor gardening, the petrified forest. It was like a bizarre modern art installation. Pots of all shapes, colours and sizes adorned most flat surfaces, containing nothing but compost, a few withered leaves and the ever-present stick. They were testament to Ann's misplaced optimism that given time they might recover. An avid watcher of TV gardening programmes she could never bring herself to believe that less might be more, a bit of benign neglect more beneficial than her overzealous regime. She greeted each death with surprise as if it had never happened before.

John checked he had his season ticket and wrapped his Everton scarf around his neck before heading off to the match – another triumph of hope over experience.

'Bye Love, hope it's a good match' Ann had learned not to plunge John into gloom by wishing the team good luck or expressing the hope that they might win. 'Don't be late. Alan and Jane will be here when you get back'.

'As if that's an incentive 'John muttered under his breath. He dreaded the annual visit of his sister-in-law and her husband. Perma tanned from their retirement in Marbella, Alan liked to give the impression that he was a mover and shaker in the criminal underworld. In reality he supplemented his pension as a cab driver and may have ferried the odd villain here and there. As for Jane, John's mother had long ago summed her up as 'all fur coat and no knickers.' John wondered if you were even allowed to say that these days. Jane's jewellery was diamante rather than diamond. Thank goodness Ann was so different from her flash sister.

He put up with the couple as best he could because he knew that Ann loved her big sister who had kept the family together when their mother had died. Jane was the eldest of five children, Ann the youngest, twelve years between them, bookending their three brothers. Once when he had suggested refusing to have them to stay, Ann, normally calm and even tempered, had exploded.

'If it hadn't been for our Jane we'd have ended up in care, the family broken up, the boys running wild. Dad couldn't have managed on his own. I wouldn't have the life I have - gone to uni, got my degree, become a teacher, met and married you, had our kids. She sacrificed a lot for us. I owe her big time. So, what, if she likes her bling and her idea of a good time is different from ours. She always did have terrible taste in men and believe me Alan is better than most of the con artists she went out with who promised her the moon and the stars before running back to their wives.'

Ann had been relieved when Jane, almost forty, had met and married Alan. She sensed that beneath his brash, pugnacious, competitive exterior there was a kind heart and that he genuinely loved her sister. For Alan, Jane was glamour incarnate – the big blonde hair, the painted nails, the high heels, the care she took with her appearance – all reflected well on him. He was one of those short, stocky confident men who has no problem being seen with a woman who is taller than him. Children were never on the agenda – Jane had satisfied any maternal yearnings bringing up her younger siblings and Alan had never felt the need to populate the planet. They were a good match, sociable, enjoyed a drink or two, life and soul of the party in their expat community.

Now the house was quiet, before the onslaught, Ann looked longingly at her book, but she needed to finish making the bed up in the pretty guest room at the back of the house overlooking the garden. She knew that Jane and Alan found it hard to understand the small pleasures of the life that she and John led, the house still bearing the scars of the rough and tumble of family life, the rooms filled with photos, books and comfortable sofas, the lack of TVs in the bedrooms. The education that Jane had fought so hard for her sister to have, had created a gulf in terms of aspiration between the sisters.

After wrestling with the duvet cover Ann opened the window and sighed as she saw John hadn't put the lawn mower away. Stopping to put the coffee machine on and promising herself half an hour with book, coffee and chocolate biscuit, Ann pushed the lawn mower into the garden shed. As she was about to secure the padlock, she heard a plaintive mew from inside the shed. Opening the door again, she peered into the dark interior and followed the sounds until right at the back curled up on some old matting, she found a small black and white kitten.

'How long have you been here? Long enough to give yourself a fright and get hungry.'

The tiny animal allowed Ann to gently pick it up. She could feel it trembling as it snuggled into her. 'Let's take you inside and get you warm '. Whilst the kitten lapped thirstily from the saucer of water Ann placed on the floor, she checked the neighbourhood WhatsApp group. She was pleased to find that there were no reports of missing kittens and reluctantly posted a message with a photo, hoping that nobody would contact her to claim ownership. After googling 'what can you feed kittens', Ann opened a tin of tuna. The kitten sniffed it suspiciously, looked at Ann as if to say, 'is that the best you can do?', ate a small amount and flaked out under the kitchen table, exhausted by all the excitement.

'At last!' Ann sighed with contentment as she poured coffee and prepared to curl up for half an hour before her visitors arrived. No such luck, the doorbell rang, and Ann was enveloped in her sister's musky perfume and the stale alcohol fumes from her brother-in-law who had clearly taken full advantage of the duty free.

'Surprise, surprise, the plane landed early for once' Jane shrieked. 'This is for you' She thrust a luxuriant peace lily at Ann. 'We know how you love your plants' she giggled.

'Love them to death, eh Annie?' Alan winked. It was one of the many habits that irritated John that Alan called them Annie and Johnnie. He refused to see it as the sign of affection that Ann claimed it was, citing it as another example of how Alan patronised and condescended to them.

Ann lovingly welcomed the latest victim. 'Do you need a hand with your bags?' she asked.

Alan shook his head 'I'll head up, rest my eyes for a bit, let you girls have a good natter. Is John at the match? Still supporting that no hope of a team, is he?'

One of the many tensions of the evening to come would be Alan comparing Everton unfavourably with his team, Arsenal. As John never tired of pointing out Alan wasn't a real football fan, seldom attended matches and then only if there was corporate hospitality on offer. Alan certainly had no understanding of the tribal loyalty of the dedicated fan. Ann was only grateful that Alan wasn't a Liverpool supporter.

'What do you want to drink Jane – tea, coffee, Lem sip?' They laughed at the shared memory of their grandmother, their beloved Nana Rowan, who had offered this to all visitors regardless of age and health.

'How about a proper drink?' Jane replied.

Ann made a token protest 'But it's not even 6 o'clock'.

'Ah come on it's always wine o'clock somewhere' Jane put her arm around her sister. 'Let's have some fun, let your hair down, relax.'

She opened the fridge and grabbed the bottle of prosecco that Ann had bought especially for Jane's arrival. A few minutes later the sisters clinked glasses and settled themselves at the kitchen table.

'What's the goss then? How are you finding retirement? How are my lovely nephews?'

Ann and John had two sons, Matt twenty-eight and Ben twenty-five. Matt worked in IT and lived in London with his girlfriend Laura. Secretly Ann hoped they would tire of life in the big city and move back north, perhaps when they were ready to have children. Ben had taken a year out after graduating and gone to Australia to work on his Uncle Pete's avocado farm in Queensland. A keen cricketer he had fallen in love with the country and was hoping to become an Australian citizen. Ann was proud of both her sons, but she missed them.

'Mmm… that's better,' Jane sighed with contentment as she slipped her shoes off, only to let out a yelp. 'What the??' She began, bending to look under the table to see what had nibbled her toes. Her face softened as she picked up the small furry bundle. 'When did you get a cat?'.

'I haven't – not yet anyway – I found her in the shed earlier. I'm waiting to hear if anyone claims her.'

At that moment Ann's phone beeped with a WhatsApp notification. Anxiously she read the message. A few minutes later she reached for the kitten who was curled up on Jane's knee.

'That was a message from the woman whose garden backs on to ours' she told Jane. 'Her cat had kittens. This is the last of the litter. I can keep her if I want.' The huge grin on Ann's face meant there was no need to ask if she was going to do so.

'What are you going to call her then?' asked Jane.

Ann thought for a moment 'Welcome to your new home Rowan.'

Jane refilled their glasses with a smile. 'Only right we should toast the new arrival, our Nan's namesake.'

A while later Alan came down looking refreshed after his nap, was introduced to Rowan and informed Ann that John would be celebrating as Everton had won, raising a quizzical eyebrow when Ann assured him that John would be heading home in time to eat with them. An hour or so and a few drinks later there was no sign of John and no response when Ann tried ringing him.

By now Ann was feeling the effects of several glasses of prosecco on an empty stomach. She realised they were all in need of food but not sure she was up to cooking anything.

'How about we order a takeaway?' Alan suggested to Ann's relief. 'You have a night off. We'll sort something out for John when he gets back if he needs it'. After they had finished their Chinese meal, they moved to the lounge to watch Friday night comedy on the T.V.

Predictably Alan piped up 'I know someone who can get you a home cinema system at a decent price. John would enjoy watching the sport'. He always knew someone who could supply the latest gadgets at knock down prices.

'Mmmh, maybe' Anne murmured peaceably.

Feeling slightly guilty, Ann realised she was almost relieved that John hadn't returned home yet. There was none of the usual sparring between him and Alan. Jane headed up to bed just before the news came on at ten o' clock, a firm believer that no news was good news.

Shortly afterwards Ann and Alan heard the sound of someone trying and failing to get a key in the lock, a muttered curse as something fell on the floor.

'That'll be the dirty stop out' Alan grinned 'I'll go. I'll enjoy this'.

'That's what I'm afraid of 'Ann said to herself.

John almost fell through the door as Alan opened it. 'Ooh, you're in big trouble Johnnie boy' Alan chuckled, rubbing his hands with glee at the mingled expressions of surprise, dismay and alarm that chased across John's face. Pasting a goofy grin on his face John thrust a chrysanthemum plant that had seen better days towards Ann.

' Sorry love' he slurred 'it was just meant to be a quick half'.

'More like a slow gallon by the look of you' Alan chortled.

'You're home now' Ann said, 'no harm done'.

'Apart from to that plant', Alan chipped in, 'it looks like you've given it a helping hand, saved Annie a job'.

John shrugged 'Sorry I wasn't here to welcome you. I'll see you and Jane tomorrow. I'll just grab a glass of water and head to bed'.

John weaved his way unsteadily to the kitchen; they heard the tap run and then 'Night all' as he stumbled upstairs. Ann and Alan exchanged a conspiratorial grin.

'Someone's going to have a sore head in the morning. Ah well, it's not as if he often has something to celebrate, supporting that team'.

Next morning Ann introduced John to Rowan, knowing he was in no position to raise objections, even if he had wanted to.

'I'm going to the pet shop to pick up supplies, make an appointment at the vet and call round with some flowers to thank the woman behind'.

'For letting her kitten wander into our shed?' John queried with a smile.

'For letting me keep Rowan of course' Ann responded impatiently. 'Don't worry about Alan and Jane. They've headed into town to do some shopping and meet old friends for lunch. If you want to make yourself useful you can clear all the empty plant pots, empty the compost into the garden and wash the pots.'

Ann told a dumbfounded John. 'And keep an eye on Rowan, we don't want her wandering off. I won't be long'.

On her return Ann was all smiles. She was pleased to see that Rowan was curled up asleep on her reading chair. Although still a kitten, Rowan clearly had a grown cat's instinct for finding the most comfortable place. 'Right, I've got steak for tea and some of that Argentinian red I know Alan likes. We need to make up for last night and give them a proper welcome'.

'Understood' John replied.

John helped Ann unload the car including food, cat toys and a basket that Rowan was destined never to sleep in. Ann made coffee for them both, motioned John to sit at the table and announced 'I've got some news. You know I said I was going round to see Jill'.

'Who's Jill?'

'The woman whose garden backs on to ours, the woman whose cat had Rowan of course.'

'Of course,' John agreed, doing his best to keep up.

'Well, she works at the cat rescue place. In fact, Rowan's Mum was one of the rescue cats. Someone had just abandoned her. Imagine. Jill brought her home to have her kittens in peace. Anyway, they're looking for volunteers. Jill's going to take me next week and all being well, I'm going to start volunteering there'.

'That's great love. I'm glad your mojo's coming back. I've been worried about you'.

'I know you have. I won't lie. I've found it hard since I retired. I don't miss the stress, but I miss the people and feeling useful, that I'm doing something that makes a difference. Thanks for clearing the empty plant pots. The place looks a lot better without them, doesn't it? I think I'm better at looking after people and animals than plants.'

'I think that's true love' John hugged her 'but I'm going to miss the petrified forest'.

When Seagulls Rest

There was an old myth at Little Crompton that when the seagulls rest on the spire of the church, something dark and evil would happen.

Little Crompton was situated on the Eastern peninsula, slightly North of its better-known neighbours, Poxton and Hambrugh. A small former fishing village with few inhabitants, it had more recently started to attract holiday makers to its beautiful lesser-known beaches and secret caves. An increase in Airbnb properties had boosted its popularity for those wanting to enjoy a more tranquil traditional seaside break.

For Lynn, this was the perfect place to bring her recently widowed, elderly father, Arthur. He would benefit from some fresh air, a change of scenery and some calmness and she would welcome the opportunity to escape the chaos of her own hectic, though disappointing daily life.

As they drove up to the cottage which was to be their home for the next couple of nights, the views were breathtaking, and Lynn felt a lump in her throat as she gazed at her dad. He looked the same but the light in his eyes had gone since her mum died 18 months ago. Her dad, who she'd always seen as so strong both physically and emotionally was a broken man – his own health had declined, and she could feel him slipping away and giving up. This break would be medicinal for them both, a chance to spend some proper time together.

The sound of the sea had always delighted Arthur, transporting him back to his childhood when they'd visit his grandparents who lived by the sea for the whole summer. The waves crashing, the call of the seagulls were the lullabies of his youth and brought a sense of calm mixed with the excitement of days to come exploring the beaches and digging for gold with his sisters.

Further along the shore in Little Crompton itself there was a general level of unease. A change in the moon's energy, which took the edge off the usual calmness the town offered. A darkness like an invisible cloud overshadowing the bay. A slight change,

67

an expectation that wasn't welcome. Locals were known to lock themselves indoors at these times, shops would close, some even choosing to leave for fear of what may happen if the seagulls rested on the church.

30 years ago, a young fisherman, a local lad, whom everyone knew as Boy Jack, had killed his parents out of the blue before killing himself. Some say he went mad; others say he was cursed. Twelve years ago, a mother and toddler drowned in the shallow waters of Little Crompton beach. Both events unexplained. Both happened after the seagulls rested on the church. The only other similarity was that all bodies were found clutching a single seagull feather. No explanation given.

Lynn and Arthur weren't the only ones settling that afternoon. One by one the seagulls strutting about the beach, turned, and headed to St Cuthberts Church to find themselves somewhere to rest on the steep tiled roof and spire. Lynn and Arthur had no idea of the myth or what was about to happen to them.

The beautiful quaint bungalow didn't disappoint from its advertised details. As they drove up the driveway, Lynn felt the stresses of the past few months melt away. She had had her fair share of challenges, but trip was about forgetting all that for the weekend and focusing on rebuilding her dad and spending this precious time together making memories.

The key was found under the lion statue as stated in the welcome email, which was reassuring and, as she turned the large silver key, she slowly exhaled and stepped inside. It was exactly as she had imagined – quirky with mismatching furniture and soft furnishings yet modern enough to have everything they would be needing. As Lynn looked around, taking it all in, she felt a weird energy wash over her, an uncomfortable presence she struggled to shake off. Her stomach flipped and Lynn assumed that she must be hungry and tired after all the travelling. So, she put the uneasiness to one side and went to help Arthur out of the car, grateful that the walk to the front door was a short one for him, noticing how much he'd aged in the past year as he shuffled the twenty or so steps.

Arthur ambled slowly to the kitchen which looked directly out to the sea with the most breathtaking views. To the right and down the hillside, you could see the village centre with its three shops, pub, post office and garage and to the right, the magnificent spire of St Cuthberts Church glistened. Arthur stared; he had never seen so many seagulls circling the church as if silently looking for prey. They weren't agitated, but seemingly calm, the majority already perching on the church roof and spire – their uncharacteristic tranquillity felt eerie and unnatural to him.

Neither Arthur or Lynn shared their uneasiness with each other, instead choosing to unpack their belongings in their respective bedrooms and then meet in the lounge to share some tea.

It was now 5 o'clock and Lynn could see that Arthur was looking tired. She had planned to cook tonight and had brought some of his favourite meals to cook.

'Toad in the hole tonight, Dad?' asked Lynn,

'Although I can't promise for it to be as good as Mum's'.

Arthur smiled sadly, the constant pain of his grief so evident in his every expression.

'That'd be lovely'.

As Arthur and Lynn settled into their temporary home and the seagulls found their individual perching spots, the village quietened, shops closed early, people retired to the safety of their homes.

Lynn woke abruptly with that same uneasiness she'd first felt when they had arrived, washing over her. She heard tapping and a cool breeze. As she opened her own bedroom door, she saw that Arthur's room was open – perhaps he'd heard it too. She walked to the kitchen and saw that the tapping was the French doors swinging open. Heading towards them the weird feeling intensified. Unease turned to panic when she saw the silhouette of her father, walking down the uneven path towards the sea. It was rocky, steep and narrow and way too dangerous for an eighty-four-year-old man to be walking down in pitch black in his slippers. What on earth was he doing?

Lynn grabbed her shoes and coat and headed to the path shouting 'Dad! Dad! What are you doing?' He didn't turn round as she had expected so she carried on walking, scrambling the final few yards or so towards him.

69

'Dad!'

The figure turned towards her and instead of the warm familiar smile of the man she had known all her life, she was met with a deathly stare, a blackness devoid of emotion. The edge of the path narrowed, the sea roiling on the rocks below as the breeze increased. The figure turned away, tripping dangerously on the sharp glint stones of the path, unbalanced.

Lynn approached Arthur and as her arm reached up to help him, she felt a hard push on her shoulders from some unknown force and she tumbled into her dad, grabbing him. There was nothing either of them could do and they then both continued to fall further and further down the cliff.

The bodies of Lynn and Arthur were found on the beach the next morning. No explanation as to the cause of their death. The only clue – they were both clutching a single seagull feather.

Enough to convince the people of Little Crompton that the curse had indeed struck again.

A Tangled Web

Joyce was up and dressed early.

She had showered and whilst drying, admired herself in the mirror. Not bad, she thought, for forty-seven.... but inwardly thinking 'who am I kidding?'

Her breasts though full and firm, were no longer pert, and her tummy was protruding a little too far, she thought. This holiday would be a great opportunity to exercise, get fit, and lose a bit of weight.

Not that David her husband would notice either way. She hoped and believed he still loved her but, since reaching his fiftieth birthday last year, he had become quiet and secretive, nothing like the man she married when she was a young innocent twenty-three-year-old and he a budding Advertising Executive of twenty-seven.

Now an older man in an industry full of bright young graduates, he was aware that his days of climbing the corporate ladder were over, and inwardly he worried about his future.

He didn't share those fears with Joyce, but instead worked even longer hours. This meant less time together, and they gradually drifted apart. Joyce had given up her career as a copywriter when David's career took off, and now she filled her days reading, going to the gym, and writing short stories, several of which she had had published.

David earned a good salary as an Advertising Account Director, so they were comfortably off. With no children, this should have been the best time of their lives, with a degree of freedom to which many others could never aspire.

However, their lives were now in a kind of limbo, drifting aimlessly, a situation she didn't like but found herself reluctantly accepting, especially as David didn't seem to want to face it.

When she came up with the idea of a two-week holiday In Rhodes, David was mildly interested.

'When were you thinking of going?' he asked her.

'Well, we need to avoid July and August as the weather would be unbearably hot.... Remember that holiday in 1979?' Joyce reminded him.

David winced as he recalled the two weeks of hell. Thinking he was young, and immune from too much exposure to the sun's UV rays, he had ignored her advice to take it easy on the first day and suffered with sunstroke which had ruined the rest of the holiday.

'I was thinking of April or May when it's cooler and not so crowded'. She paused and waited for his reply.

'Well, I'd love to come, but we've got major client reviews so will be pretty well tied up most of April and May. But I don't want you to miss out so it's probably best to go on this one without me. There will be other opportunities......'

He was happy for her, and whilst she was sad that he had so quickly passed up a chance to re kindle the spark in their marriage, she was resigned. In fact, inwardly, she was excited.

The holiday they had in Rhodes in 1979 was not quite the disaster she had made it out to be. It was during that holiday she had met Dimitri, the handsome son of the Hotel owner. He was a couple of years older than her, bronzed by the summer sun. Attentive, interested, and interesting, he was a welcome distraction, and with David in bed most of the time, she enjoyed having Dimitri as her companion during the day.

For his part, Dimitri was attracted to this pretty young English woman, and the fact that she was married didn't seem to bother him one bit. Joyce fell for his charms, and they enjoyed a brief but passionate affair that glorious summer.

So, she had booked the same hotel they had stayed at back in 1979, after establishing that the same family were still the owners and Dimitri was now the General Manager.

Her heart beat a little faster at this news, and briefly allowed herself to imagine their reunion after twenty-one years.

Then told herself to stop being silly: he was probably married with a family and wouldn't even remember her.

In preparation for the two weeks she was going to be away, she made sure there were plenty of David's favourite meals in the freezer, and asked Marie, her next-door neighbour and best friend to keep an eye on him while she was away.

Marie was a single woman of similar age to Joyce. Her husband had passed away suddenly leaving her with a young daughter to bring up by herself. She had done a wonderful job thought Joyce. Saffron was now a beautiful young woman of twenty-five, at the beginning of her career with a prominent law firm in the city.

Joyce waited in the front room of their detached house, ready to embark on her solo holiday.

She left in the taxi. She didn't notice the curtains at Marie's front room windows open slightly.

Marie was excited. She didn't have too many opportunities to spend time with her lover.

She and David had started their affair a couple of years earlier; it was one of those cases of a friendship which turned into attraction. Marie was old enough to know that this was not love, but not having had a man in her life for many years, and never expecting to meet anyone now, she was surprised at how giddy she felt whenever she saw him and how much she looked forward to spending precious hours with him.

Initially she felt guilty, after all, he was married to her close friend. However, as the affair developed, the guilty feelings evaporated, and she gave herself totally to her lover.

Time together was precious. He was married and although her daughter was now living independently in her new apartment in the city, Marie still saw her regularly, ensuring that their mother-daughter relationship was not compromised.

Meanwhile, Joyce arrived at the hotel in the late afternoon. The Hotel was very much as she remembered, located on a secluded hillside, ideal for a relaxing holiday. It had a private swimming pool, a small gym and a yoga platform that overlooked the shimmering blue Aegean Sea. A perfect place to rekindle that holiday romance.

At the reception, she looked around for Dimitri, as a rather portly man with thinning hair came out of the Office to welcome her. There was no mistaking him, those same piercing blue eyes. It was Dimitri. However, he had not aged well. Fortunately, there was no glimmer of recognition from him, and she said nothing but later as she unpacked her suitcase in her room she felt sad, the sadness you feel when a love affair ends. She sighed and put her thoughts of what might have been behind her.

Stop being a silly middle-aged teenager she told herself 'I'm happily married to a wonderful man, I need to focus on what I have, and not some stupid romantic dream'. Joyce spent the rest of the holiday swimming, toning her body, and looking forward to returning home with a determination to rebuild her marriage.

It was after 9.00pm before Marie took a long soak in her bath, put on her makeup, slipped into a negligee, wrapped a long coat round herself, took Joyce's key from the key rack, and quietly left the house.

Letting herself into Joyce's house she crept quietly upstairs. As she tiptoed across the landing, she heard girlish laughter coming from the bedroom. And hesitated, puzzled.

She opened the bedroom door.

David was lying there naked, and beside him, the naked figure of her daughter Saffron.

A Day in a Life

I turned the small silver coloured lock and slid open the heavy, large glass window. Immediately the sound of the crashing waves came into the room and I looked down to see the white foamy sea. It was sweeping towards me as if it was charging inland with huge intent, the waves leaping into the air at varying heights.

The swirling noise of the breakers, stopping and starting, was a welcome sound. It felt fresh and alive, the waves living and moving, a source of food and life for the birds swooping down, allowing the seagulls to rest as they sat on and rode the tide. I imagined the droplets of water, flung in the air by the strong current and their salty taste.

I thought about leaving my room, taking the lift down the six floors to the ground and walking along the tideline but I would need to dress first and I felt too weary for that. I turned round and pressed the switch on the black enamel kettle, full of water and sat waiting for it to boil.

'Ready for a cup of tea or do you want one of those dreadful coffee capsules?' I asked Bill

'Err, a tea please' was the curt reply. It was not intentionally curt, but Bill was busy. He had work on his mind as well as a long to-do list, targeted for completion today, before it built up again.

The tea was hot and welcome. I was thirsty, my mouth had felt dry from the moment I had woken up. It was a familiar feeling. The night air was always warm and made me wake feeling dehydrated. Bill drank his tea quickly in silence, continuing to work at his laptop, a hard frown on his face, in full concentration on the brightly lit screen.

Unusually, I had had a good night's sleep and there was little on my mind. I sat still, cup in hand. I had moved through the glass door onto the small balcony and was listening to the sea. The wind swirled the top of my hair around gently as if caressing my head, carefully cooling me. I could see the sea clearly through the Perspex screen that served as a protective boundary between my seat, the sea ahead and the ground below.

I continued to sip the hot tea until the white china cup was empty and then, rising from my seat, I left the balcony and returned into our room.

I dressed. It was a careful choice, taking into account the weather and my mood. Nothing tight, just cool, natural cotton with a loose feel. I needed to feel free and alive, so I chose a pale blue colour gingham patterned dress, loose fitting and midi length. Sunglasses and a natural weave bag complemented the look.

This was the second day of our visit. The break, a week in total, had been carefully planned, for a special celebration. We also wanted to enjoy some good weather, warm and sunny relative to the usual windy, cloudy conditions at home.

Finally dressed and refreshed with the tea I decided to go for a walk. I hadn't thought particularly about my final route, but I was keen to explore the beach and its ever-present tide to the south. That was the view I had enjoyed looking out to the left of the apartment.

I would be walking on my own as Bill continued to work quietly, his phone buzzing intermittently and with his laptop now plugged into its charger. I didn't want to disturb him.

'Just popping out, heading down Orange Avenue via the beach. Just round the area we spotted when we drove in on Thursday. I'm looking forward to listening to the sea close up'.

'Sounds great' said Bill without looking up from his screen. 'don't forget we said we'll explore the park with the Victorian bandstand. Looks like there's going to be a Festival on there we can go to while we're here this week.'

'Yes, I'm looking forward to that, especially if the weather holds.

'I'll join you later, yeah?' Bill turned round and blew me a kiss.

I set out into the sun and placed my speckled framed, dark shaded sunglasses over my eyes. I looked up at the bright blue and cloudless sky, pleased that my new tan leather flat sandals felt comfortable on my bare feet as I strode along the sea front.

The roar of the tide filled the air. The salty, seaweed smell filled my nostrils, and I breathed in deeply. There were a couple of small children playing on the pure coloured sand, its fine grains having been swept by the tractor and its accompanying riddle, sifting the stones and rubble every morning. As a result, the beach looked perfect. The children giggled, building sandcastles as their mother pulled brightly coloured toys out of their buggy style pram. They were already covered in sand at such an early hour of the day, and it made me smile to see them playing.

'Hi!' shouted their mother as she turned to pull the toys out of the pram.

'Morning' I shouted in return, 'lovely day!'

I quickly realised that I was in a popular area for early morning joggers, carefully having to dodge them running towards me as well as overtaking me. Young people in bright coloured Lycra joggers and sweat tops, speeding by, their high stepped, specialist sports trainers giving them the comfort their feet needed as they hit the concrete path, pace after pace. Other more novice, careful runners in search of some easy exercise passed by more slowly with painstaking expressions on their faces.

I turned into Orange Avenue just a few yards inland of the beach. It was already bustling with traffic, and I stopped at the pedestrian crossing obeying the clear, automated voice instruction to 'Wait'.

I could see across the road that there was a sign advertising a book sale and I checked the date. It was today and it was at the library, the modern, single-story brick building opposite. The smell of fast food and strong coffee hit me as I crossed the road. There were rows of stalls, books stacked by genre in clear plastic crates. A coffee stall was in a shaded rectangular courtyard surrounded by clean white plastic chairs and tables.

I took off my sunglasses, exchanging them for my reading glasses and walked slowly on the dry, crispy grass to the bookstall clearly marked 'classics'. There were books of raging styles, red hard backed from the 1930's, a mix of more recent publications in colourful covered paperback form as well as hardback books with worn spines and dogged eared pages.

I picked up a copy of Aesop's Fables which had been a favourite of mine as a child. I knew I had a colourful hard back copy that my father had bought me, but this was an even older copy. It was a large A4 style hardback in monotone grey with a dramatic illustration of Aesop's characters on the front cover. I decided that would be a good purchase. I added to my purchases a new writing journal which was very prettily wrapped in clear cellophane and ribbons.

'What a lovely mix of books' said the grey-haired lady on the pay desk 'I didn't see these when I went round before, or I might have grabbed them for myself.' She smiled.

'Thank you' I replied paying for the books in cash.

There was no sign of Bill and I decided to stop, sit down and have an espresso with a slice of homemade banana bread from the coffee stand.

I could feel the relief in my tired legs as I lowered myself down onto the hard bench and putting my sunglasses back on. My rest soon broken when I heard a voice.

'Hi, I love your dress'. I looked up. A petite, blonde haired female in her 50s with a newly bought coffee in hand was busy sitting herself down close to me.

'Where did you get it from?'

'Oh,' I said, surprised 'it's a well-worn one, a favourite of mine!'

'Well, it's lovely. My name's Joi. I'm busy campaigning today on the stand just outside the library – forthcoming election in mind and lots of work to do. Pop over and see us!' She stood up to return to her stand nearly spilling her coffee as she moved away.

I stayed at the coffee stand for a while watching the crowds before venturing across the road to check out the park Bill and I intended to visit. It was busy but I could still hear the sounds of the birds singing on the sunshine filled the air. Sitting down gratefully on an unoccupied old iron seat I opened my book and, losing myself immediately in the story, time passed quickly.

I hadn't heard from Bill so I decided I would walk back to the apartment, carrying my books in the blue canvas library branded bag that I had been given with my purchases.

The sun was shining brightly, and I noticed that it caught the diamond bracelet I was wearing on my right wrist. It was sparkling, a long chain of small square set diamonds. I stopped and stared at it. It was like it was speaking to me. I thought back to four months ago when Bill has surprised me, despite us being together for over thirty years, telling me that he had decided to buy me a gift of jewellery for our anniversary. It was to be special, and I could choose.

We had visited a renowned jeweller to look at rings and my ring finger was measured (I can't remember my size I was too excited!)

The choice of fine cut diamond rings with their thick gold and silver bands was vast. I was mesmerised.

Measured up and spoilt for choice we had left the jewellers and crossed the city by taxi. We chatted excitedly on the way and arrived at another jewellers - this was the jewellers where we had bought our wedding rings and my engagement ring and so it was special. The aged, helpful manager who had carefully assisted us with the choice of our original rings was no longer there having retired long ago. The new, young staff, however, were equally helpful. They pointed out a diamond bracelet, snake shaped, with pure square designed diamonds in a continuous shiny silver link.

'You choose' Bill said lovingly. Looking into my eyes 'your choice. Love you'

I felt spoiled. I needed some time to think so we went for a walk, stopping for a drink at a trendy bar whose customers spilled onto the street in the sunshine. We talked and chatted quietly, each in our own thoughts.

I finally decided to choose the bracelet. It was gorgeous, very special being from our original jeweller. Bill had been so thoughtful, and I was now lovingly staring at it again, so grateful.

Arriving back at the apartment Bill met me with a big, warm hug.

'Work all finished, I'm changed, freshened up. Ready to go out when you are.' He said.

I was still keen to get out again and explore with him despite just getting back to 'base'.

'That sounds great. Wasn't expecting you to be done. I'll get changed now.'

I changed as quickly as I could. I had a dress in mind and slipped into it, a beige 1930s style silk dress that was fitted round the waist and came to a perfect length.

'Ready. Let's go and hit the town!' I said.

We meandered through the town, hand in hand chatting, glad to be back in one another's company then headed over to the beach once again.

'We're here' said Bill suddenly sparking into life. He held my left hand tightly with his right.

At the sun-drenched restaurant, we were directed to a table for two by the large window, overlooking the seafront. The waves were still crashing, welcoming us, loud and fresh. The slim, tall, dark hired waiter appeared and took the drinks order.

'A French 75 please' I said, looking forward to my gin cocktail.

'A small beer for me' said Bill 'A local IPA if you have one'.

We waited for the drinks, chatting about the day. The drinks arrived.

'Cheers, darling' whispered Bill. 'This is for you. From me. I love you'.

I looked down. He had in his right hand a small crimson box which he opened.

'For you.' he said again.

I was speechless. In front of me, in Bill's hand, was the ring I had been measured for.

'For you, darling' he said.

'It was supposed to be a choice of one or the other' I replied, feeling completely overwhelmed.

In silence, Bill moved to place the ring on my finger. It was like nothing I'd seen or felt before. It was huge cut, the ring, digging into my skin, feeling heavy, strangely new and also alive. Just like us, I thought, it reflects us.

'For you' said Bill again 'this is about us'. We giggled as a wave suddenly splashed against the glass screen.

'Wow!' we shouted together laughing.

'Thank you so much. I love it!'

I had never felt happier. Bill had surprised me so much and we kissed. At last Bill was thankfully, relaxing. His priority was us, and I knew that it always would be.

I looked forward to returning to our apartment, listening to the waves breaking again on the beach and turning the small silver coloured lock to close the heavy, large glass window.

I knew that I would have a very good night's rest that night, after a particularly special and memorable day.

Great Expectations

Men, bless them, seem to think that when their wives are engaged in an activity that does not involve them, most of the conversations will somehow manage to include them. I'm a member of a female only book club, and the one occasion I can recall any mention being made of husbands, was when we were reading, 'Great Expectations', and Greta Conroy, after a few glasses of red, came out with.

'Well, we'll be no strangers to them, show me a woman who's not started her marriage   full of them and ended up with her dashing, gallant beau up to his oxters in beige and cultivating fuchsia.'

There was much nodding of heads in recognition of this immutable male development arc.

This evening, I had proof positive that the process was well underway in my own relationship. Larry had just spent the best part of our twenty-fifth wedding anniversary dinner mansplaining the vital importance of cheese cultures in stamping the characteristics of particular cheese types. He reached a crescendo, with a comparison between Cashel Blue and Stilton.

'It's with regret that I have to concede that Stilton beats Cashel hands down in the blue cheese stakes. But then it's been around in a form we'd recognise since 1720, plenty of time to get the cultures right, Cashel's late to the race, a novice.'

'You've always loved your Stilton, Larry. An sure Cashel's coming on leaps and bounds, I'll put the coffee on, love.'

As the beans were grinding, I thought of the first time I set eyes on Larry. He revealed himself a bit at a time, a dance of the seven veils. Shaggy head, hair to the shoulder, a short nap of stubble below the high cheekbones. Army surplus jacket, decorated with anti-Vietnam War badges and other causes close to his heart, washed out Levi's, feet shod in suede Veld boots. He was climbing the stairs of a front-loading double-decker bus. I was sitting three seats back from the top of the stairs, in the window seat, eating a sausage and chip supper. He flopped down beside me.

'Give us a chip Miss, please Miss, just one, go on Miss, givus one.'

'Have a sausage to go with it, why don't ya, ya cheeky ghet.'

Somewhat taken aback, and shocked he looked me in the eye, 'I never eat pig flesh.'

Then launched into a tirade about the cruelties of the meat trade, pointing to a badge on his combat jacket which screamed, 'Meat is Murder.'

To take some of the heat out of the encounter, I changed the subject to what we were doing: he, studying 'A' levels at a college of Further Education, having been booted out of the sixth form at a local Jesuit school. Me, studying photography at the Art College.

Nearing my stop, sausages uneaten, we made a date to meet in the Adelphi Bar for a drink, then on to Sammy Houston's Jazz Club. Some band named Them, led by a fella called Van Morrison, he thought, were playing, he didn't know if they were much cop, got the tickets from one of the bouncers, his brother knew.

It was a memorable night, the band were great, did a fabulous cover of 'House of the Rising Sun', all melodiously bluesy. Larry left me home and we knew there would be other evenings. What sealed it for me, provided his credentials as the most romantic man I'd ever met was a summers day a few months later, we had arranged an outing at Shaws Bridge.

He turned up in a green linen jacket, sporting a battered Panama hat, and carrying a small leather case into which he'd crammed a litre of Nicolas Vin Ordinaire Rouge, a French baton loaf, some camembert, an anthology of love poems, and a travel rug. He called this assemblage, his Pre-Raphaelite Kit.

The afternoon was glorious, warmed by the sun and wine, we lay in the long grass and reeds near the river's edge, he read some poetry, lines from Auden's, 'Lullaby', remain with me:

But in my arms till break of day
Let the living creature lie,
Mortal, guilty, but to me
The entirely beautiful.'

Kingfishers overhead: flashing fluorescent blue fireworks, the fragrance of meadowsweet draped on the air….

'Maura, are you growing that coffee out there?'

'It's nearly done love; you know how temperamental this old thing is getting.'

'Alright, when it's done'.

He'd had a few pieces published in the Honest Ulsterman, showed great promise according to Frank Ormsby, but then me expecting with Ciara, the temporary teaching job, Christ, he was now the assistant- head. I think it was my photographs being picked up by the media, described as, 'capturing with a gritty, realism, the essence of the troubles', then the exhibitions in London and Dublin. He was very congratulatory, but…

'Maura…'

'I'm coming love'.

Walking into the sitting-room with a pot of his favourite Italian coffee, and Shaws Wafer Thin Mints, I put the tray on the table. Pour a cup for Larry, take a small bite from a

wafer thin mint and stretch out my hand, holding what remains, towards his mouth. His lips slowly part to receive it. I bend over and gently kiss the growing tonsure on the crown of his head.

Epiphany

Ben stoops to pick up Ellie as he does every evening. His precious little daughter. He carries her to the tall glass doors and points down the long garden to the first-floor windows of the house whose garden backs on to theirs.

'Tell me what you see.'

'The curtains are closed, Daddy. Does that mean the little girl and boy who live there have gone to bed?'

'It does, and what does that mean?'

'That it's my bedtime' Ellie announces with all the authority of her three years, enjoying the familiar nightly ritual.

Ben smiles and puts her gently down. 'Let's go and say night night to Nana and Grandad first.'

Ellie trots happily into the next room and runs first to Grandad Steve and then to Nana Sue to kiss them goodnight.

'Do you want me to take her up son?' Ellie's grandmother asks, 'you look tired, and you need to be off soon.'

'Thanks Mam but it's ok.'

'Come on now lovely, up the apples and pears we go' Ben says, holding the door with the creaky hinge open.

Grandad Steve says, as he does every night, 'Must give that some oil tomorrow' whilst Nana Sue rolls her eyes humorously and intones 'which never comes.'

After a quick bath Ellie puts her arms up so that Ben can lift her out and wrap her in the soft towel he has warmed. She sits on the saggy old wicker chair that Nana insists on keeping and whilst Ben dries her feet he sings 'This little piggy went to market' causing her to wriggle and giggle until they get to the part about the little pig crying 'wee wee wee' all the way home.

'When will we be going home Daddy?'

Ben pauses, holding her extra tightly, breathing in the sweet scent of her newly washed hair.

'Soon, lovely, soon,' Ben soothes.

Ellie brushes her teeth and Ben helps her to put on her pyjamas, the ones with the characters from Robin Hood on them, then chases her to the back bedroom, Ellie giggling as she jumps into her bed, all part of the regular nighttime routine.

She knows that Daddy used to sleep in this bed when he was little and she feels safe and secure as he tucks her in, not too tightly. The other bed lies empty, where Uncle Harry slept when he was a child.

'It's time to say your prayers and then we'll have a story' says Ben, reaching for a book on the bedside table.

Ellie shuts her eyes, putting her hands together, a picture of piety for all of twenty seconds. Opening her eyes and smiling at her Daddy she begins

'God bless Nana and Grandad, God bless Daddy, God bless Mummy and God bless Jack.'

Small as she is, she is sensitive to the shadow that crosses her Daddy's face when she prays 'God bless Mummy and God bless Jack.'

Ellie's bedtime story is all about how Robin Hood and Little John met in Sherwood Forest. Her favourite too soon finished.

'One more story' she begs.

'It's time to close your eyes and go to sleep now.' Ben says, trying to be firm. He stands up.

'Pleeese' she persists.

Laughing, Ben shakes his head. 'If you go to sleep like a good girl, I can't absolutely promise, but there might be a lovely surprise for you when you wake up in the morning.'

Resisting her entreaties as to what that surprise might be, Ben draws the curtains so that the room becomes dim, bends to kiss Ellie's cheek and goes, leaving the door ajar so that she can see the light from the landing.

Ellie lies in bed wondering what the surprise might be, and if there will be a surprise at all, because Daddy had said he could not absolutely promise.

She thinks about her baby brother, Jack, who is being looked after by Uncle Harry and Aunty Louise. She remembers how disappointed she was when they brought him home from hospital and told her she had a brother. She had so wanted a sister. Is that why Jack is living with her uncle and aunt, where is Mummy, is it her fault they are not all living at home together?

If Ellie tries hard, she can remember the wallpaper on her bedroom wall at home. Although it is dingy, it is pink and has neat rows of red roses. She likes the colour, and she likes the order of the neat rows.

She tries her best to stay awake as long as she can, dreading the bad dreams that invade her sleep every night, especially the one where she and Mummy are on a crowded bus and become separated – Ellie at the back of the bus, Mummy at the front.

In the dream the bus climbs a steep bridge over a canal. As it reaches the top the bus splits in two. The front of the bus with Mummy continues, the back of the bus with Ellie falls into the canal. Eventually tiredness overcomes Ellie, her eyelids droop, close, and she sleeps.

When Ellie wakes next morning, the sheets are wound around her and her hair is plastered to a damp forehead, signs of another fitful night. She is glad to see the light leaking in round the corners of the curtains where they do not quite fit the window.

It takes a moment for her eyes to adjust and to realise that the monster on top of the wardrobe is only a pile of boxes. That does not explain the breathing that she can hear.

Ellie turns over to face the other bed, which should be empty but is not. There is a large lump under the bedclothes, a large breathing lump. It can't be Daddy because he sleeps next door in the little bedroom. Her skin prickling with fear Ellie opens her mouth to scream but, as in her dreams, no sound comes out. Then the lump changes shape, becoming huge as it rolls over. Ellie shuts her eyes tight and holds her breath.

'Ellie,' a voice whispers, 'are you awake?'

Cautiously Ellie opens her eyes and looks straight into the smiling face and outstretched arms of her mother.

'Mummy' she screams and scrambles out of her tangled bedclothes and into the warmth and love of her mother's hugs and kisses. Her small body suffused with happiness, a never to be forgotten moment of pure joy.

Rock, Paper, Scissors

'You're going to be a dad' The words almost winding me, crashing into my stomach like that time in Year 9 when the school bully Kurt Shipley punched me for my dinner money.

'Wha….? How…...?' I managed to stammer, which was received with an 'I think you know how' glance and a raised eyebrow from Holly.

'But… I thought….' I blurted, frustrated with myself for being unable to finish a sentence.

'I know, me too, but I guess accidents really do sometimes happen' said Holly seeming to understand me despite my difficulties in getting my words out.

I looked at her, my girlfriend of less than a year and, although I did love her, I hadn't ever thought she was the one I'd settle down with. I wasn't ready to commit to one person for the rest of my life. I still fancied Tammy who worked at The Frog and only yesterday the girl on my daily commute I'd secretly fancied for the past 5 months turned back and smiled at me before she got off at South Sheers.

'How long?' I asked Holly trying to disguise my fear which I had figured was paralysing my vocal cords and limiting my articulation to only two words at a time.

'I'm eight weeks tomorrow' she replied. My brain quickly calculated that in 7 months' time, before next Christmas, I was going to be a dad. Jesus. We didn't even live together. My job paid an OK salary for one person still living with his parents but wouldn't stretch far for two and certainly not for two plus a baby plus rent. I started to sweat, and my heart was racing. I didn't want to ask the obvious question for fear of upsetting Holly but a child at twenty-two, really? This was not part of my plan. I had a lad's holiday with the football team in July which I'd been saving up for and work had talked about a three-month project abroad. Shit! How could this happen? I felt my life crashing down before me.

I'd met Holly on Tinder and didn't really fancy her at first, but we exchanged a few messages. I'd also been messaging this beautiful girl called Claudia who had ended up ghosting me and my heart was bruised. Then randomly on a night out with the lads – I'd bumped into Holly in Sparkles, the only nightclub in Riverhampton. We never usually went there but it was my mate, Lemon's birthday and as we were all staying at his house, we'd gone out locally. She was prettier than her profile (or maybe it was the beer?) funny, sexy and we really hit it off. We had a drunken snog before I vomited in the toilets and Davey T helped me back to Lemon's house.

I woke up the next morning with a hangover from hell and a message in my DMs from Holly. It was a photo we'd taken the night before (I could barely remember) and a 'great to finally meet you' text. We arranged to meet up the next week and ended up having one of the best dates I'd ever been on. I think because I didn't totally fancy her, I could just be myself and it was just so easy.

We played this game – it was basically rock, paper, scissors and the person who won got to ask any question they wanted. It was a bit of fun and I soon found out that we supported the same football team, both liked red wine, Oasis and had played hockey at school. It wasn't much to go on, but it formed the basis of our relationship and here we are eleven months later about to be parents together! Oh God! I'd let my mind wander and had almost forgotten….

'Rock, paper, scissors?' asked Holly. We'd continued the game throughout our relationship. I nodded. Determined to win, I went in hard with a rock. Holly played paper.

'You always go for rock when it's a difficult issue, paper when you want my advice about something and scissors when you want to lower the tone and ask something naughty' I smiled at how well Holly knew me.

'So' she asked tentatively 'How do you feel about it?'

I looked at her face, full of worry and nerves and wanted to say something to reassure her and make her feel better but our deal with the game was that we always spoke the truth, our naked truth.

'Scared, terrified, shitting my bloody pants'.

Holly smiled, 'Me too' and suddenly at that moment I knew I needed to man up and do the right thing and be there for Holly and this baby.

I think it was when we had our first scan a month later that I started to feel this bubble inside me. Instead of the anguish about how I'd miss out, how I'd cope, what would people think etc, this felt different. Once I saw the blurry outline of this living thing that somehow in a moment of passion we'd created, this bubble of excitement, joy and happiness was there, and it was there to stay.

I started to get carried away and imagine taking him to his first football match. We didn't know the gender yet, but I was convinced it would be a boy. We talked about names – I liked strong names like Thor and Goliath (Holly wasn't as keen). I was determined that I would teach him to swim and found myself googling when babies could go to the pool. Life was changing for us; plans were being made and I couldn't wait. I was on cloud nine and that bubble of excitement just continued to grow and grow. Until one day it popped.

I got a call from Holly to say that she had taken herself to the hospital as she had been having cramps. She'd also started bleeding. At this point she didn't know what was going on but there was a chance that she was losing the baby.

I felt like I was in a fog – I rushed to the hospital on autopilot convincing myself that she'd be fine, he'd be ok, but it was clear as soon as I saw Holly curled up on the hospital bed, red eyes and looking devastated that we'd lost him. I honestly felt like I lost a part of me too. The pain and grief of losing someone you've not yet met, don't even know what they looked like is indescribable. The gut-wrenching agony of lost hopes and dreams is too hard to explain. This was heartache as I'd never felt before, the raw ache of grief.

But I had to be strong for Holly. We held each other while she cried, and I tried not to. She'd never seen me cry before and I didn't want to start now.

She stayed in the hospital overnight whilst I went home. Everything felt strange and things looked different – greyer, less bright, empty, and meaningless. The next few months passed by

– some days I really struggled to get through, other days I momentarily forgot.

I did end up going on my lad's holiday and I also taking up that three-month project in Brussels with work. Holly and I broke up a few months later. I think we both knew that it wasn't meant to be for us. I texted her on his due date to let her know that I was thinking about 'Goliath' and that made her smile.

This experience changed me. I still think about him and imagine how old he'd be, how my life would be. I'd never thought about kids before but now I just know that when it's right, I can't wait to be a dad.

Sour Grapes

'So, what do you think?' said Penelope with that haughty, superior tone that she adopted to imply that her knowledge of wine, or indeed anything else, was greater.

Sheila took time to savour the wine.

She had to admit, this was a delicious, full bodied mature Malbec. She savoured its almost velvety smoothness as she let it wash round her mouth.

She didn't have much in common with Penelope. They had been in the same year at Junior School 30 years ago, and only met recently at the Wine Club, of which, of course Penelope was President.

Penelope hadn't achieved that position through her extensive knowledge of wine, but rather through her wealthy husband whom she persuaded to underwrite the cost of the whole year's wine stock. Penelope believed that money and position could buy you everything.

She had lived as an Au Pair in France after school, having neither the desire nor the qualifications to enter University.

Sheila on the other had worked hard and won a place at a top University, where she studied Modern Languages, and after graduating, spent time in France, Germany and Spain in a variety of vineyards learning all about wine, before returning home recently to take care of her elderly parents. There were limited opportunities, so she took on the job of Librarian. It suited her, the hours were flexible, and fitted her domestic commitments.

The Wine Club was a good opportunity to enjoy wine and meet new people, so she willingly joined, even though the subscription and monthly wine events were a little expensive for Sheila, whose income as a librarian was modest.

While Sheila joined because of her love of wine, Penelope was a member because of the social side, the many opportunities to network, talk about her wealthy lifestyle, and impress everyone.

They had grown up in the same village gone to the same junior school, and then grammar school. It was there, aged 13, they had fallen out at an end of year party.

Shelia liked a boy called Geoffrey. He was a nice quiet shy boy, so they were suited. They were getting on quite well, when Penelope moved in, or tried to. She wasn't popular, but her parents were well off, so she used that to attract boys.

The village hall had been decorated especially to look like a disco, which was the fashion then. A giant silver ball hung from the roof, the light reflecting across the room as the ball rotated to the beat of the latest hit.

Sheila and Geoffrey were dancing on the edge of a crowd of their friends, when Penelope moved in.

She tapped Geoffrey on the shoulder. 'Hi Geoffrey' Penelope said, completely ignoring Sheila.

'Great moves' she gushed. 'Want to come to my party on Saturday?' 'All the gang are coming. It will be so cool....'

Poor Geoffrey. He didn't know what to say, croaking out a mumbled. 'I guess so '.

'Great .... I'll see you then'. Penelope turned to Sheila, smiling triumphantly.

'Night Sheila. Enjoy the party! '

94

With a goodbye wave to Geoffrey, she flounced off.

Sheila, hurt and humiliated walked off, leaving Geoffrey standing there alone.

Outside the hall she wiped away her tears and ran all the way home. Sheila didn't see Penelope again until that Tuesday at the Wine Club. Sheila recognised her immediately, and the pain of that memory came flooding back.

Penelope seemed to have no memory of that night and smiled graciously to see Sheila amongst the guests. It was during the meeting after the usual small talk, that Penelope suggested the two of them should have a wine tasting of their own. A time to catch up on old memories, but inwardly she saw it as an opportunity to impress Sheila with her beautiful home, and of course her extensive knowledge of wine.

'What do you say Sheila? It will be fun. Come round to mine and bring your favourite Malbec; we will each taste the other's choice and decide which is best for wine and value. '

Sheila's initial reaction was a reluctance to have anything to do with this vacuous woman who had hurt her so many years ago. However, she put that aside, seeing this as an opportunity to get even.

It was quite the most elegant and stylish home Sheila had ever visited, curtains carpets and drapes in perfect balance and sofas with deep cushions to sink into.

She had to admire Penelope in one way; she had snared a very wealthy man, and clearly enjoyed the lifestyle that went with it. She had met Gerald while working as an Au Pair in Switzerland. He was a Merchant Banker and a prime target for the upwardly mobile Penelope.

'Do tell me what you honestly think!' Penelope continued, her voice loud and confident.

'Isn't it just the best Malbec you've ever tasted? '

Sheila paused, letting her mouth appreciate the rich fruity flavour. 'It certainly is very good'. 'I would say it is definitely a French Malbec '

She said this confidently, knowing that Penelope would never buy any wine that wasn't French.

'Right first time' exclaimed Penelope with delight. 'You can't beat a French Malbec - can't you just taste the French grape, the heavy tannin combined with the fruit giving it that vibrant fresh taste, so unique! '.

'You've been reading the wine critics again' Sheila teased.

'No, I haven't' Penelope snapped back, defensively, knowing she was lying and not having any sense of humour where her self-image was concerned.

'I just know my wine' she continued, implying that she knew more than Sheila. 'Let's sample yours then' she carried on stiffly, confident that her Catena Alta would surpass anything Sheila could offer.

Sheila poured a glass of her Pierre Jarrant.

Penelope raised the glass to her lips, breathing in the heady aroma before taking a sip. She had to admit to herself that Sheila had exceeded expectations. This was a full bodied fruity, vibrant, and refreshing Malbec. A simple fluke she thought, either that or it had cost her a fortune. Much more than someone like Sheila could afford.

'So, what's your verdict?' asked Sheila pleasantly.

Penelope put down the glass, breathed deeply, reaching a consoling hand across to Sheila's arm.

96

'My dear, I quite understand that your financial situation is, shall we say, more challenging than mine '

'What do you mean, more challenging?' Sheila was furious, angry at the condescending tone and insulting inference, that Penelope as somehow superior just because she lived in a large, detached house and had more material wealth, while her own lifestyle was more modest.

'This is an excellent wine' Penelope tried to calm the atmosphere, patting Sheila's arm patronisingly. 'Obviously expensive. I didn't mean you to overextend yourself, you know…. financially. I'm sure there are ordinary wines out there….'

Sheila quietly removed her arm from Penelope's grasp. 'You know the price of everything and the value of nothing. Since you clearly know so much about wine, let's reveal the price we paid.'

'Okay Sheila, mine was a Catena Alta and cost £33.99 from the Wine Club' she replied smiling triumphantly. 'And yours?'

Sheila raised her glass, studying the deep colour of the wine. 'Oh…' she said carelessly. 'This was a Pierre Javant from Aldi, priced at £4.99'.

She smiled pleasantly at a stunned Penelope. 'Cheers' she drank deeply.

The silence was deafening.

Home Truths

A wave of sadness washed over Maurice as he loaded the last For Sale board into his van. Retirement had finally crept up on him after 20 years working for Prestige Estates. Not that there was anything 'prestige' about his job, not according to Gloria anyway. Putting up For Sale boards for a living didn't really rank on Gloria's job snob scale. Maurice knew that she told people he was in 'Real Estate' and the lovely cottage in the village he had inherited form his father gave her plenty of status locally. Although he gave her a good life it irked her that he still hadn't put her name on the deeds giving fuel to her resentment about his job, and she ridiculed him about it at every opportunity.

Maurice pulled up at his first stop, 22 Sycamore Drive, and hefted the board into position on the front lawn. To the likes of Gloria, it was just another board but to Maurice it was much more than that. For twenty years he had been putting up these boards, or signals to the world that the lives of people were about to change for better or worse.

Take Sycamore Drive for example. A beautiful Georgian four bed detached in half an acre of gardens. The house was being sold because Geoffrey White, local solicitor and womaniser extraordinaire had been caught by his wife for the third time in a compromising situation with the bar maid at the local golf club.

The For Sale sign signalled the end of a fifteen-year marriage and endless misery and humiliation for Geoffrey's wife. Gloria should give that some thought, having a good job meant nothing if you weren't a decent person.

Maurice moved on to his next stop, 12 Beech Close. A small semi-detached at the head of a cul-de-sac. As he fastened the 'Sold' label to the board attached to the gatepost Maurice felt like he was putting up a sign that shouted 'yes at last' to the world. Janey and Sam had lived there for fifteen years. For ten long years they had tried for a family. Cycles of fertility treatment had put a huge strain on them but just as they were about to give up Janey fell pregnant. The baby was due in three months.

With an offer accepted on a larger detached house in the next road the board was letting everyone know it was time for them to sell up and move on to a new chapter in their lives.

Next up was 4 Acorn Court. Not such a happy sign for this flat. Old Mister Jenkins had passed away two months ago. He had been a great character in the village, stalwart of the Bowling Club and mainstay of the Britain in Bloom Committee. His two daughters who had, between them, seen their father for the grand total of twice in the last three years had wasted no time in getting the flat on the market. Maurice had liked Mister Jenkins who had never failed to ask 'how's that stuck up woman of yours? Still with her?'

Maurice moved on to his next to last house, 25 Chestnut Crescent. The rambling six bed detached was set in five acres of landscaped gardens and boasted of a tennis court and swimming pool. Maurice bashed the spike post hard into the front border.

This was a sign for justice. Leon Cooper had lived here for the last five years, strutting round the village like Lord of the Manor. Now he was strutting round a cell in Wandsworth prison after his life of money laundering and drug dealing had come to the attention of CID. Gloria had often embarrassed herself simpering around Cooper but for some reason she had gone very quiet on that front now.

Maurice pulled up outside his last house of the day. The last house of twenty years in fact, 13 Laburnum Crescent. A quaint chocolate box cottage that was one of the oldest in the village. Not too big but certainly not poky, it nestled in its well-tended gardens and boasted a stunning view of the village green and duck pond. The cottage had been in the same family for four generations and the For Sale sign would signal the end of an era, a complete and utter severance with the past.

Maurice hoped this house would go to a young family who would bring the love and happiness back that had been missing from its four walls for some time now. Maurice hammered the 'For-Sale' board into the border next to the garage.

From this vantage point Maurice looked down on the village that had been his home for the whole of his life. He could see the school playground where he had played football and conkers with his pals, the scout hut where he had learned to make a fire by rubbing sticks together and the alley behind the shops where he had his first kiss with Martha after the school disco. He could also see the spire on the church where he had married Gloria. Full of hope for a happy life with a couple of kids, Gloria had seemed so sophisticated, and he couldn't believe she was interested in him. As the years went on Maurice realised that perhaps it was his family standing in the village that had been more of an appeal to Gloria than him. When no children appeared she had implied that it was a failing on his part but then one day Maurice moved the dressing table out to put a new electrical socket in and found a packet of contraception pills that had fallen out of the back of Glorias drawer. Things had never been the same since that discovery.

He pulled open the garage door that had been left unlocked and moved aside some sacking, to reveal the large suitcase he had put there that morning. He wheeled the suitcase down the path and took one last look at his rose garden before he loaded the suitcase into the van and pulled away without looking back.

He wished he could stay around to see Gloria's face when she came back to find the cottage for sale, but he had a long drive ahead. Annie had already moved down to the cottage in Devon he had bought three months ago and would be waiting for him with a nice casserole in the oven. He wondered if Gloria would put two and two together when she saw an advert for a new receptionist at Prestige Estates, but he didn't dwell on that for long.

There's a Stranger in my House

Even before I smelt the spicy aroma of Thai curry, something didn't feel right as I put my key in the door. It was as if my sixth sense had kicked in before my mind had even a chance to keep up. I couldn't say why, but something just felt weird. Not only was I always home before Jack, but in the two and a half years we'd shared a house together in Tooting Common, I'd never known Jack to cook. Ever. Plus, unlike me, he hated spicy food.

'Who's the latest girl *you're* trying to impress?' I joked as I kicked off my fake Manolos that had been digging into me all day and hung my French Connection wrap-around coat or rather I balanced it on our wobbly coat stand, a skill I had mastered over the past few months after Jack had found the wooden stand at the tip and assured me he could fix it.

I headed straight to the kitchen. Our house was small, some may say '*bijou*'. Downstairs comprised a lounge to the left, stairs to the right and a kitchen straight ahead. Two medium sized bedrooms upstairs and a bathroom.

'… and what are you doing back so….' I started, opening the kitchen door. Instead of being greeted by my red-headed six-foot one flatmate, I was met by a slightly shorter, older looking bloke wearing a buttoned up stripey blue shirt and suit trousers. He had an earring in one ear and had a very tidy beard and looked very at home in our kitchen.

'Hi, I'm Brett, you must be Sophie. Didn't Jack tell you that he had to go away for a few days, and he had said that I could crash here?'

Stunned by the sight of a stranger in my house as well as annoyed at Jack for thinking that I would be OK with this and not giving me advance warning, I hesitated before actually replying.

'Sorry?' I said, 'you're a friend of Jack's?'

'Yes, we go way back, old school friends. He must have mentioned me before.

This was really unlike Jack. He has always been a considerate flatmate. Quiet when he came home late, even if he was drunk. He would always call ahead if he was bringing someone back with him. Jack's lack of washing up skills was about as bad as it got with him.

Something didn't quite add up. Brett looked older than Jack, the telltale signs of ageing beginning to emerge –white flecks in his beard, a receding hairline and laughter lines which seemed to persist long after the joke had been told. But if he was a friend of Jack's I didn't want to appear rude, so I excused myself, deciding to call Jack and get the full story.

The familiar sound of Jack's voice asking the caller to leave a message was not surprising – he never answered his phone so I quickly sent him a WhatsApp message and told myself not to worry, Brett seemed nice enough and I was sure that there would be a good explanation as to why Jack had forgotten to tell me about this visitor. But I still couldn't shake off an uncomfortable feeling that something wasn't right. Still, it had been such a long time that a man had cooked for me, that I decided to override these niggles and accept, enjoy the meal and deal with Jack later.

When I went back to the kitchen, there was something oddly familiar with Brett that I hadn't picked up on before.

'Have we met before Brett?'

He smiled. 'Sadly not. But I have heard a lot about you from Jack' The way he said this sounded creepy, but I forced a smile. One of the side effects of living in London - we'd undoubtedly passed each other on the commute, it happened all the time – strangers passing, the occasional glance, not even acknowledgment, then never to see them again.

Brett opened the drawers and located the corkscrew in the second one. He had already found the only two decent wine glasses we had, the ones we usually saved for guests. These were stored at the back of the cupboard so he must have really rummaged to find these. As he released the cork, Brett's eyes didn't leave mine, smiling triumphantly as it popped.

His eyes continue to stare at me as the wine poured into the glass.

I was absolutely gasping for a drink and could smell the oaky aroma of the familiar Merlot. However, something was telling me to keep a clear head.

'Cheers' he said, lifting his glass and nodding from me to the glass he'd poured.

'Sorry I er... don't actually drink red wine' I said, rather unconvincingly.

Brett looked despondent, almost irritated. 'But you *will* eat with me' he almost ordered.

Startled by his demand I stuttered 'Of course' and watched the tension in his face started to soften.

'How long are you staying for?' I asked, trying to sound casual.

'A... a few days'

'And sorry but *where* did Jack say he had gone to?'

'Does it matter?' and his annoyance began to flare up again.

'No, I just wondered as he doesn't usually take off without telling me'.

'I don't know, he just said that I could stay. That's all. You OK with that?'

I smiled, reassuringly although I suspected that the sincerity didn't quite reach my eyes.

His demeanour seemed to change to tense and angry when questioned about Jack. If they were friends – what was upsetting him?

'I'm just going to change out of my work clothes' I said trying to act casual, putting aside my discomfort and headed upstairs. I sneaked into Jack's room searching for luggage that might indicate how long he had planned to stay but strangely there were no bags in the room. Except Jack's 'man-bag' the gift I had given him last Christmas. He'd laughed when I gave it to him but was soon barely seen without it and marvelled at how he could now carry his wallet, phone, keys and even a small bottle of water with ease.

Wait – what was it doing here? Hadn't Jack taken it to work this morning? I tried to think if I'd seen him with it as we left to catch our respective trains. It was just possible that he had left it here, but I really couldn't be sure. The daily grind of the commute meant that every day seemed to roll into one and you barely noticed the little things anymore.

I was just about to look inside it, hoping that I wouldn't be met with a mouldy half eaten sandwich when I heard Brett,

'It's ready Sophie' so I left quickly changing into a more comfortable pair of jogging pants and a baggy jumper.

We sat down and ate. I was feeling weirdly ill at ease in my own house with a stranger who had cooked for me. How bizarre. The food was quite delicious.

'This is really good', I commented, with an approving nod.

He smiled, his eyes hovering over mine as I ate, making me so nervous that I began to struggle to eat much more.

'You haven't eaten much', he observed, frowning as I pushed my plate away.

'I guess I'm not really that hungry. Sorry.'

We cleared the plates away together, awkwardly skipping around each other in the kitchen. I made my excuses planning to head up to my room and stay out of his way for the rest of the evening.

'But I thought we could watch a film together'. Brett complained as I made to leave.

'Sorry I've got some work I need to do for an early meeting tomorrow.' I fled, leaving Brett stony faced at the sink.

As I headed back upstairs to the sanctuary of my bedroom, I felt my heartrate increase as Brett appeared at the bottom of the stairs. I turned, beginning to panic.

'Just heading upstairs, myself,' he called up with a reassuring smile. I managed a casual smile back.

Safe in my bedroom, I looked at my phone. The WhatsApp message I'd sent Jack earlier had not been read but there were two missed calls from Esther, Jack's colleague from work. Were they away on this work trip together? She'd left a voicemail.

'Hi Sophie, it's Esther. I'm afraid Jack has been mugged. He's OK but he's in hospital and he's lost his phone, so he asked me to call you to let you know he'll be staying in hospital tonight. He may need picking up from Guys in the morning. Don't worry he's going to be OK; they are just keeping him in for observation'.

What? That didn't make sense. Why did Brett say that Jack had gone away with work? My head was swimming with confusion, my heart pounding with distress.

A wave of panic hit me. I felt vulnerable and scared. Who the hell was in the room next to me? How did he get into my house and what was I going to do?

Terrified now, I texted Esther back *Does Jack have his keys with him?*

No came the immediate reply *They took everything.*

Everything

Yes, he's gutted that they took his bag – you know the one you bought him for Christmas.

Adrenaline took over then and I put on my trainers, grabbed a coat, my keys and phone and ran out of the house, phoning 999 as soon as I could.

'999 What's your emergency?'

'There's a stranger in my house.......'

Plus One

Giles and Ella had relocated to London from Scotland with work several months ago and all was going to plan. They had found, what was for them, a perfect house, one they could expand into. Giles had brought his beloved BMW estate or 'the Limo' as he had fondly named it and they had made some friends in their neighbourhood. Giles had been relieved to find his new work colleagues welcoming. The job was a challenging one, but he thrived on a challenge. His team had a collective cheeky sense of humour, teasing him hard about his Glaswegian accent. Work involved long hours in the office and resulted in very little time generally for socialising.

Working lunches were the norm, and, at such a lunch, during discussions detailing the efforts required to achieve the demands of their current project, they were surprised to be joined by Georgia, fondly known as the' big boss'. Georgia sat down confidently perched on the end of the bench. She was known for her straight talking, hard work ethic and no-nonsense approach to her own style, both with work and how she presented herself.

Georgia usually kept her personal life to herself, so it was a surprise when she announced, with huge excitement, that she was getting married. She usually showed little emotion, but she was clearly delighted at this happening to her. Something that she had apparently never expected.

She had met Darren only 6 months ago and, with no reason to wait, they had decided to get married. In just two weeks' time. Work forgotten for once, she happily discussed her plans for the wedding, becoming animated when outlining the carefully scheduled arrangements.

Smiling, she announced to everyone, 'You must come to the wedding!' Amid murmurs of surprised assent, she turned to Giles. 'And you must come too. You're a key member of the team after all, and I would like you to be there.'

Giles, taken aback, agreed. 'Of course. Thank you.' He hadn't expected to be invited, being such a new member of the team.

Georgia grinned, Giles' response was obviously what she had wanted to hear. 'You're very welcome.' She turned back to the rest of the team.

'I'm sure you'll all be pleased to hear that it's on the Saturday, so no need to take time off work,' she smiled round at the expectant faces, who grinned back ruefully.

'It's in the Park and the service will be conducted in the pop-up Chapel by the Serpentine. By the lake. No presents required and there are no formal invitations so don't expect one in the post!'

Giles' listened carefully, sure to take in all the details.

'Oh,' added Georgia 'bring your plus ones – they're invited too'.

That evening, back home, he casually mentioned the invitation to a surprised Ella, who hadn't expected a formal wedding to be her first introduction to Giles' boss and work colleagues. She hoped she would fit in; her background was in education not the commercial world and she felt nervous. How would she be received by the unfamiliar London corporate world?

Ella found the lack of detail and information particularly unhelpful.

She and Giles has married within a short period of time too, but they had managed to issue invitations, had spent a fortune on flowers and all the other usual wedding paraphernalia – which she now admitted was mostly down to her mother who had insisted. Perhaps Georgia didn't have a mother like that, or anyone to support her.

But Giles was delighted that they had been asked and so, after her initial unease, Ella said nothing and set about finding the perfect outfit to wear to impress. She lost count of the number of dresses that she tried on, imagining excitedly returning home with a glamorous outfit wrapped up in tissue paper in a designer bag. Instead, she managed, or so she thought, to be realistic or 'keep a perspective' as Giles suggested, trying to contain his wife's increasing desperation at her lack of success. Eventually a suitable outfit was found. Giles liked to think that it had something to do with him presenting his credit card and telling her firmly not to return home without something wearable. The search had gone on long enough!

With the help of a very patient, experienced and older personal shopper in a large London Department store Ella had selected a damson-coloured dress. It had a fitted bodice, empire style, a lace trim and a flared skirt. The personal shopper had decreed firmly that high heels were not suitable and so Ella had invested in a pair of nude coloured ballet pumps offset by a similar colour, gardenia-ordained, clutch bag. The outfit had met with the approval of the many ladies in the department store who had gathered round Ella to assure her that damson was the in-colour and, in their motherly way, that she looked beautiful.

The day of the wedding came round quickly, and, with an early start, Ella was up, dressed and ready. She admired Giles, dressed smartly in his suit with his recent newly styled hair. Ella knew he would help her through the day. They set off in the Limo driving to the Park's Serpentine entrance arriving just in time to walk into the temporary wedding chapel. It was bustling with guests, and it took them a while to find their seats.

As she sat down Ella felt hot and uncomfortable. She wondered if the choice of dress material was too thick, or perhaps it was her nerves. She shuffled up to Giles who was looking about distractedly, a smile fixed on his face. He nodded and turned to wave at a familiar face as Ella whispered that she needed some air and slipped away.

Safe then in the cool tiled interior of the Ladies' room she splashed her face with welcome cold water, taking in some much-needed deep breaths. Perhaps she really shouldn't have come. She sagged against the washbasin, overcome with tiredness.

The door swung open, a sudden clatter of sound from the guests milling outside, then a quiet snuffling noise.

Ella turned, surprised to see the bride, Georgia, crying as she closed the door. She was accompanied by a small flower girl around eight years old, who began to pull faces at herself in the mirror, clearly bemused by the upset.

The little girl glanced at Ella through the mirror. 'Your dress is like mine. Are you Georgia's friend? Are you expecting a baby?'

Georgia looked up, her face pink and crumpled, 'I'm sorry…' sniffing. 'I'm not normally like this…. I don't know who you are …'

'I'm Giles wife, Ella. Are you okay?'

Georgia wiped the tears from her cheeks, trying to pull herself together. 'You must think I'm mad…. my wedding day and I'm like this!'

'Not at all. Nerves can get to all of us.' Ella replied soothingly.

'My sister, Cicily, is sick. She was to be my maid of honour but…' Georgia paused, staring at Ella.' That's strange…That dress you are wearing. It's almost identical to hers, the colour is perfect. How did you know?'

'Know what?' Ella looked bemused.

'The colour palette I'd chosen for the bridesmaids! You could be one of my bridesmaids…. actually…' Georgia took a deep breath 'would you be my maid of honour, would you take Cicily's place? Please? I'd be so very grateful…'

'But I didn't know about your colours' protested Ella 'this was just the most forgiving dress I could find. I'm pregnant and feel horribly self-conscious. I can't possibly take your sister's place…I don't know you!'

'Please' whispered Georgia, sagging against the wall, almost defeated. 'You look beautiful. And it would mean a lot to me.' She straightened up, took a deep breath, and went in for the kill 'and I like Giles. I'm sure he'd want you to help me out' giving Ella a meaningful look.

Ella understood. And remembered that she had wanted to make a powerful impression on Giles' colleagues. Maybe this was how to do it.

'If you're sure, then… yes.' she agreed.

Georgia smiled, instantly recovered, and turning to the mirror coolly began to repair her smudged make up.

Ella felt in a daze. She couldn't believe what she had just agreed to do. She wondered if she was in a dream but found herself and the flower girl following Georgia swiftly to the entrance to the Chapel where the guests were waiting. This was for real.

'There's Darren' said Georgia, nodding to a tall figure standing in front of the registrar 'he's waiting for me.'

Ella looked down the aisle at the groom, who felt her gaze and turned towards her.

'You…' he mouthed silently, in disbelief. He stared hard at Ella noticing her blossoming shape, turning pale, as the wedding music began.

It was Ella's turn to cry.

Chosen

They say once a human imprints on a dog's heart, they are there to stay. I always thought this could only happen with one person and I'd had my person. And then I didn't – he'd become so much a part of my heart, that I'd almost depended upon him for it to beat. When I lost him, I lost myself too.

'What about this one?' I heard a young lady ask as she passed my cage. I didn't look up, but instead slunk as far back into the cage and lowered my eyes. She smelt good - of summer days and happy times, of walks in the park and special treats.

'He's broken' said Isaac, who ran the shelter. 'I've tried so hard to reach him but he's going to take a lot of work'.

'What's his story?'

'Abandoned. We found him a few weeks ago. He was a bit malnourished but otherwise had obviously been well looked after. A bit shut down so we're thinking he's been through some kind of loss or trauma'.

'He's beautiful,' said the young lady.

'How about this one instead?' Isaac directed the lady to Zack, one of the cutest pups in the shelter with big floppy ears and excitable eyes.

'He is very cute, but…. I don't know, there's something about this guy.' I closed my eyes even tighter, terrified she would take me away. But she didn't. She stayed by my cage and just sat there.

After a while I allowed myself to glance up and look at her face. She had the kindest eyes I'd ever seen but I sensed a sadness within her too. A sadness that echoed mine. We dogs feel emotions deeply – we know how humans are feeling often before they do, and I could feel that this person was 'broken' too.

She came every day that week and just sat near my cage. After a few days. I began to trust her and took the treats she offered. I allowed myself to look at her again. This time as our eyes locked, I knew she was my person. She took me home that very day and it wasn't long before Claire was imprinted in my heart, and we became each other's whole world.

We did everything together. We'd go for walks on the beach, have baths together, movie nights at home, I got to sleep in her bed despite her telling me that it was 'just this one-time'. I loved her and she loved me. I was so happy.

But there were times when I allowed my brain to drift back to my previous life and Claire would ask what was wrong, like a huge sadness washed over me. Because the truth is that I did have a life before Claire. I had another owner and thinking about him made me sad.

Jim got me when I was a puppy, he trained me, disciplined me, and kept me for almost seven years. He was my whole world and when he was at work, I waited at the door for his return. One day he came back, and I sensed that he was in a bad place. His eyes had a faraway look, and his smile was gone. We left the house that night with just a bag and spent the next few weeks roaming the streets. We had each other for warmth and Jim always managed to find me food and take care of me the best way he could. Until one day, he was gone. I looked for him everywhere – I followed his smell all around the city until there was no more trace, and I didn't know what to do. That's when I got picked up by the dog warden. He was kind to me and gave me lots of yummy food, a basket to sleep in and he promised me that he'd find me a home. But I didn't want a new home, I wanted Jim.

Weeks passed and still no sign of Jim. Lots of people came to the rescue centre looking for their new pet but I just looked away, cowered in the corner, refusing to engage. But then came Claire. My wonderful Claire. But oh, how sometimes my heart still ached for Jim. When Claire is around, she helps my heart but when she's not, I must try really hard not to think about Jim otherwise I'm worried it might stop beating.

Claire's heart was full of love and kindness. But she too had a sadness about her. I didn't know why or what had happened, but Claire knew I sensed this, and we would often sit and cry together, sharing yet not understanding each other's pain. She would look at a photograph of a man on a motorbike, I would have to remember Jim's face in my head.

Every Tuesday evening Claire and I would volunteer in a homeless cafe. I thought of it as a bit like the shelter where I was at. I could feel the sadness and despair emanating from all the different people. I saw them as lost, damaged souls without their person and place in life. I soon learned that I could help them by just sitting with them, allowing them to feel and offering them some warmth and comfort. I loved it and they loved me.

One day I smelt a familiar smell in the shelter. We dogs smell before we see, and each human has a unique smell to us. That smell was engrained in me, the most beautiful smell, attached to my person. It was whisky and apples and leaves and oak trees. It made me think about happy times playing ball and warm winter evenings snuggled on the sofa. I followed the smell to a very dishevelled, older looking Jim.

The regulars were used to me being a calm and gentle dog and were surprised when I leapt on top of the unsuspecting new member who was sat quietly in the corner. As our eyes met, his sparkled with tears,

'Bobby. Oh Bobby, how I've missed you son!'

I licked those tears away and put my head on his lap. This felt like coming home. My heart was healed. He sat stroking me and I could feel the sadness in his soul begin to melt.

Claire appeared.

'Barny – get down! I'm sorry, he's never usually *this* excited to see anybody!'

I looked from Claire to Jim. She smiled, the kindness overflowing from every pore.

'Is this your dog?' he asked her.

'Yes, he sure is. The best.'

What? I was confused. Tell her Jim, tell her…. I nudged his hand.

But Jim just smiled back at me, stroked my head and made an excuse to leave. I tried to follow, but someone shut the door behind him. I'd lost him again and my soul and my heart were crushed.

Then something happened. A miracle. Jim came back the next week and the week after and, well I got to spend time with him again. He laughed, we played, and slowly he started to look alive again. He and Claire started to talk to one another, and his eyes began to smile once more.

113

Then one day I saw it. That look in their eyes. It was a different kind of smile from Jim, a lingering look after he'd left from Claire. She began to spend longer getting ready, sprayed that awful perfume on her that I think humans like when her natural smell was SO much better. I knew she was starting to look out for Jim's arrival.

He also started to look better. Firstly, it was a neater beard, then a haircut, better clothes. All this along with the spark in his soul, meant that my Jim was actually a very attractive man, and this had not gone unnoticed from Claire.

Claire helped Jim get back on his feet – letting him know what he needed to do, where he could go for help. But mostly by believing in him. She saw what I saw.

Jim never did tell Claire that I was his dog beforehand, but that didn't matter. It didn't take long for Claire and Jim to fall in love and the three of us became a family. Claire tells everyone that I helped her find her soulmate and when she does, Jim winks at me. I am the luckiest dog in the world with my two people by my side.

A Date Worse than Death

Tammy curled her red hair round her index finger nervously whilst trying not to look at the door to the bar. She had deliberately chosen a table with a direct view in the hope that she would see him before he noticed her. Her friends nicknamed her 'fifty first dates' as she had been on the dating apps since she'd broken up with Steve last summer. She had strategies, a no-nonsense approach and prided herself in sniffing out the red flags immediately and moving on to the next one. However, she was feeling surprisingly anxious about this one and wasn't sure why.

Tammy had only really swiped right on his profile because of the picture of him with a dog. Not that Tammy was a huge dog lover, nor did she have one of her own, it was just that she had decided that men who liked pets had a softness and compassion to them that she was searching for. Obviously, that did not extend to fish. That was an automatic swipe left. She scoffed at her own naivety but when that's pretty much all you had to go on plus a few words that generally meant very little, these things were telling.

Tammy stirred her coffee for the tenth time. She always arrived at dates early – partly so she didn't feel too exposed on entering. There was nothing more awkwardly embarrassing than trying to work out which one was your date on arriving at a quiet bar alone. She'd learnt that the hard way and cringed when she thought about some of her early dates when she'd almost fallen into the bar pushing the wrong door, or that equally embarrassing entrance when she'd tried to enter through the fire door. Tammy was not what you'd consider, or at least what the city of Manchester considered a cool, trendy lady. She was pretty in a girl next door kind of way, yet clumsy and slightly awkward.

She perched his book on the table. Clinton Wells was a published author. As an aspiring writer herself, she couldn't help but be impressed with that. He had ten books published where she struggled to write occasional short stories. The dedication and focus that must take was inspiring. She'd googled him, bought his book and all this alongside the banter and wittiness portrayed in his messages had really got Tammy's heart racing. More so than any other guy she'd chatted with and there had been a lot. She'd even shared some of her writing with him. Clinton also seemed kind and interesting. He had had his heart broken too – had felt the devastation of infidelity like she had, and his vulnerability had sealed the deal for her. He flirted enough to keep her interested but never crossed the line into vulgarity. She was keen to meet him and wasn't afraid to let him know. They hadn't spoken on the phone or video-messaged but that was OK. It was only a meet up in a bar, a first date and she knew how to keep herself safe.

It was approaching 7.30pm and Tammy glanced up again at the door as a couple, clearly in love, walked in. The man had his arm affectionately on her shoulder as he held the door open for her. They sat in the window, laughing and gazing into each other's eyes. Tammy looked on with envy. That's what she wanted. She'd never really had that with Steve. She felt sure that Clinton would be different. Tammy was forever the hopeful romantic. However, there was still no sign of him. She exhaled loudly, enough for the lady in the couple to glance around. Tammy had an impatience towards tardiness and a two-drink rule. She would stay for a second drink and then leave.

There was only one other guy in bar – an older man in his fifties with an untidy moustache, and glasses, dressed in a shirt and tie drinking a pint of beer. Tammy sniggered inwardly wondering if he was waiting for a date too.

A sinking feeling came over her as her mind wandered amidst the fear that maybe this guy was masquerading as Clinton Wells. She'd heard about catfishes before on dating sites and although Tammy had often been surprised at how unlike their photos some of her dates were, this had never happened to her. However, she dismissed this thought and reflected on all the discussions they had had about the characters in his novel that only an author would know. But still something about that thought sat uncomfortably with her.

Noel Symmonds sipped his pint and looked over at the girl with the beautiful red hair and luscious lips. She was very attractive and alone. He never had any luck with women and didn't quite understand why. He still lived with his mum, but his

116

recent promotion meant that he might now be able to afford to move out. He decided to take the plunge and say hi. Besides, she looked lonely.

'I've read that book' he said as he approached her table 'He's a great author'.

'Err yes' said Tammy clearly trying not to engage.

'Do you mind if I sit here?' Noel asked, pulling out the chair and sitting down before Tammy had the chance to reply.

'I'm actually just about to leave' she said, as she stood up and put her coat on. 'Sorry'

'No problem' smiled Noel and Tammy couldn't help but notice the stained smile with the missing teeth. She could feel his eyes on her as she got up to leave.

Tammy left the bar before she finished her second drink, but it was now 7.34pm and he should have been in touch if he was running late. As if on cue she heard her phone ping.

Sorry, lost track of time. I'm on my way heading down Parrs Lane. If you're still in the bar, wait there, if you've given up on me and are heading towards the station, hopefully I'll meet you halfway there. X

She smiled. Ever the optimist. As Tammy headed towards the station, eyes peeled for Clinton, she failed to notice Noel leaving the bar and heading in the same direction.

Parrs Lane was quiet for a weekday evening and Tammy couldn't see anyone walking towards her. Her heart sank once again as she realised that it probably wasn't going to happen.

Disillusioned and disappointed she decided to head home on the tram and turned into the small alley which led to the station, checking her phone one last time. As she put it back into her coat pocket, Tammy felt someone grab her from behind, their hand clasped over her mouth before she had a chance to even comprehend, let alone make any kind of noise. Her eyes had been covered with something and she was pulled in the opposite direction. Fear spread across her body like blood pooling from every area. She felt paralysed and helpless as she was dragged into a van, tied up and driven away. Everything happened so quickly that Tammy had little time to notice anything or even compute what was happening.

They hadn't gone far when the van stopped, parked up and the doors were flung open.

'Get out!' the voice said, pulling her by her arm. Tammy tried to notice what she could, the stale smell of beer on his breath, the strong Mancunian accent telling her to get up. The way he grabbed her by the arm suggesting he wasn't particularly tall.

She was led up some stairs into a dark room and thrown to the floor.

'Stay here' he ordered.

Tammy was petrified yet surprised to notice the smell of incense and cleaning products, the warmth of the heating, soft luxurious carpets. It felt clean, expensive, far from where she was expecting to be.

'Now. Tell me exactly how you are feeling right this very moment.'

The voice was soft, yet gravelly. It felt strained even when speaking quietly.

'Who are you? Where am I?'

'I'll explain later, first of all, I want you to describe your thoughts.'

'Err... scared, terrified, confused, ...' stammered Tammy.

'That's great, now tell me what you think is going to happen to you?'

Tammy was now even more confused. What was going on? The way he was demanding the questions, told her not to argue and she didn't have time to think of alternatives.

'I don't know, are you going to hurt me? Keep me here?'.

'This is great. Now what words would you use to describe how you are feeling?

'Petrified, disorientated'

'Disorientated.... Excellent' and Tammy could hear the soft tapping of keys on a laptop.

'What do you want from me?'

'You're helping me'.

'Helping you, how?'

Just then she felt him, come nearer to her and he pulled the mask off her face. Squinting through the changes in light she recognised him at once and felt even more confused.

He saw her being bundled into the van before he had even finished his cigarette. Even though Noel wasn't much of a runner, he followed the van into the cul-de-sac.

'Clinton?' Tammy was shocked to see that the guy she had been messaging all this time, was real.

'Nice to meet you!'

'But what's going on, what was all that?' she asked, 'Is this supposed to be some kind of joke?'

'I never joke'.

'But….' Tammy's mind was racing, and she glanced around thinking about how she was going to get out of this situation. Her hands were tied, and he was in between her and any obvious escape route.

'Don't even think about trying to escape. The door is locked'.

He looked like the photos she had seen of Clinton, but the spark she had detected in his eyes was gone and replaced by a darkness, a coldness that sent icy chills through her body.

'What do you want? What's all this about?'

'Research. I need to understand the character in my new story'.

Tammy was baffled and even more afraid. She'd read some of Clinton's books and knew that they were violent and graphic and not something she wanted to have a starring role in.

'I'm struggling to empathise with the character I'm writing about, and I want to know how you feel, being captured. What are your thoughts?'

'What the…….?' She began to shake, her body involuntarily trembling from fear.

Clinton noticed. He smiled.

'This is good. Now any other physical symptoms?'

Tammy felt sick and could feel the bile rising from her gut. But wasn't going to let him see this and decided to challenge him.

'I feel nothing except pity. I thought you were a talented writer with the ability to empathise into the complexities of the characters you portray. But really, you're a joke'

Clinton's face angered and Tammy feared that she had overstepped a line.

But her inner strength continued to rise replacing the bile she previously felt.

'And how does this end, eh Clinton? Are you going to kill me like you killed Jessica in *For Our Sins*? That ending was so predictable'.

'That would be too easy' he hissed, and his eyes narrowed Tammy suddenly felt very vulnerable, her earlier bravado morphing into fear.

'I have a different plan for you' he smirked 'You're a talented writer, Tammy – you're going to help me finish this novel'.

Clinton came towards Tammy with some scissors and Tammy froze, convinced he was going to stab her or cut her throat. But he carefully took a lock of her hair. This was almost even more terrifying. The serial killer in Clinton's last book always kept trophies of his victim's hair.

'Now how fast is your heart racing?'

'Pretty fast' she whispered.

'Describe how else you feel physically.'

Tammy realised that if she had any hope of escape, she would need to appease Clinton and do what he wanted.

'It's almost like my heart is going to beat out of my chest, my hands are so sweaty I feel like they are going to slip away, and the blood has been drained from my legs so that there is now no feeling left there at all'.

'This is great Tammy' and he tapped out the words verbatim onto his laptop.

'And if I told you that I wasn't going to kill you, but beat you up so bad, you would wish you were dead?' He said almost clinically.

This is so messed up thought Tammy wanting to tell Clinton that she was thinking about how she would try and grab those same scissors and ram them into his throat.

'Err Tammy?

'Sorry?

'I asked how you would feel if I told you I was going to beat you up so badly that you might wish that you were dead?' he repeated, as if he was asking her a question in a job interview about how she might respond to an office disagreement.

'I'd be frozen, paralysed to the ground, unable to speak. The only movements would be the thoughts of my loved ones in my head playing like the credits at the end of a film'.

'Excellent' he continued to tap away.

How was this going to end Tammy thought? she just had to find a way to get out.

Just as she was thinking about how she could convince Clinton to let her type, the doorbell rang and before he had a chance to gag her once again, Tammy screamed 'Help! Let me out of here, I'm tied up!'

Clinton grabbed the scissors ready to threaten her with them as they both heard someone trying to kick open the door.

As Noel forced his bodyweight against the locked door for the third time, he felt the door begin to crack and eventually pushed it open. He heard her screaming.

'Let her go!' He shouted. She was shaking.

'Leave us alone!' Clinton shouted. 'Or I'll use these' nodding to the scissors in his hand.

'Put them down and let her go' said Noel softly.

Clinton looked at Noel, realising that he wasn't going to give up and his face began to look defeated.

'I'll let her go on one condition. You don't involve the police'.

'Why shouldn't we?' said Noel.

'Just let me go and I promise I won't say anything.'

'Are you sure you're ok with this?' asked Noel to a petrified Tammy.

'Just get me out of here. I just want to go home' He put his arm around her as he turned to Clinton and said,

'You promise you won't come after her again?'

'Of course not, now just go and please leave me alone!'

Noel ushered Tammy, shaking through the broken doorway. She was so grateful to this man for saving her.

'I'm sorry I was rude before in the bar. Thank you for everything you have done for me, you've saved my life' she hugged him.

Noel beamed. 'Is there anything I can do to repay you?'

'Maybe we could meet up and have that drink another time?'

Tammy looked at this unlikely hero with his wiry moustache and yellow teeth.

'Of course, I'd love to but right now I just need to get home' and she gave him her number.

As they walked away, Noel hailed down a cab to safely get Tammy home. He smiled and waved as the taxi drove off.

Just then his phone pinged.

The things I do to help you get a date!

He replied,

Thanks mate. Hope you got the research you needed!

After Sun

Jacqui had been elected Mayor two years ago. At first this was a cause for celebration, she liked being in the public eye, doing her bit for the community and, as she said, fulfilling her role in public service. She fought hard to be elected and conscientiously worked at her profile culminating in her success. Her celebratory speech concluded with her emotionally declaring,

'I am delighted to have been elected and I truly thank you for your support – I will do all I can for this area, your town.'

The audience had responded warmly with loud applause and supportive cheers.

The last two years had brought her in contact with a huge number of people. She had attended events that she had never knew existed prior to being elected, had gained a mayoral car with ribbons, a team of staff and a huge workload especially the in boxes of correspondence regularly received from the residents of the local area.

'I have perfected the handshake' she was known to cheerfully admit at functions and was delighted when this simple statement raised a laugh, which it usually did.

She was used to being reported on at the events she spoke at and faced a full diary, booked months ahead. It was difficult to take any time out, to get any form of break in her schedule.

'Perhaps we can just get away somewhere, you know, together' Peter, her husband quietly and hopefully suggested when Jacqui had recently asked him what he would like for his birthday. Jacqui had sighed in response and frowned.

'I know, I know' she replied, 'let's see' and, quickly changing the subject, added 'How was work today, was Cath in the office causing her usual unrest?' Jacqui was distracted, thinking about the heavy burden of Office, her promise to see the Mayoral role though and the realisation that the demands were too much at some times that she didn't hear Peter's reply to her question.

A scheduled change in routine the following week saw Jacqui driving herself to her office. She made her way slowly through the heavy traffic, nimbly meandering through the queues in her bright red Mini Cooper. The Mayoral car, a large black Jaguar, was being spruced up for an important forthcoming event. She looked out of her car's small windscreen, a contrast to the Mayoral Limo's windows, and set the equally small windscreen wipers working to clear the spots of rain that had begun to fall and smear the glass in front of her.

She was soon lost in thought with the melodic whirring of the wipers. She shivered in the cool, damp car waiting for the heaters to take effect and longed for some warm air to reach her through the small vents. Her thoughts moved quickly to what Peter had said and knew that he longed for some sun. She smiled at the thought. It was unlike him; in fact, she could never remember him wanting to 'get way' in the autumn or winter months but it sounded like a perfect idea just now.

The journey to the office was a slow one in the wintry weather and heavy traffic and she was tired and weary when she arrived. Her walk reflected her mood as she pushed open the heavy wooden door, laptop case in hand. She paused as the noise of the ever-busy Mayoral Office washed over her. The phone was ringing and Fiona, the Head of Staff, was answering a number of queries

'Yes, that's all fine. I'll make sure Jacqui is there. It will be no problem for her, I'll clear the diary'.

As the call ended Fiona rushed over to Jacqui and explained that there was to be a high-profile visit from a VVIP and Jacqui would be needed. Jacqui listened as she took off her long navy-blue overcoat and wondered who they were referring to. She heard herself wearily mutter out loud 'Oh no, oh dear' wondering whether the visit would involve a particular organisation – a new one or one she had been involved with before – probably one with its own particular rules and procedures to be carefully followed. She hoped it wouldn't be one like that and she ached for some creativity for a change.

Plans were revealed as the day went along and Jacqui felt unsettled and, unlike her, almost uninterested in the forthcoming visit.

'Is the deputy Mayor available instead?' she had uncharacteristically asked, and, with raised eyebrows, her Head of Staff told her that it was Jacqui who must attend.

She was unsure why she had little enthusiasm for the event. Maybe it was the weight of the work, the routine or the never-ending issues and arguments she had to deal with. These weren't just those in the office but were much wider – across various groups and parties and, oh, those clashes of appointments. Once she had thrived in this type of environment, not now though. She didn't know and she really didn't care, not today anyway.

The week continued and Jacqui counted the long days. The following week was packed with meetings, too many 'all dayers.'

'We've a conference on next week, Jacqui' her secretary had firmly stated 'should I have your official outfit dry cleaned as usual?'

'Yes', Jacqui had simply replied wishing she could have used the equally simple word that had the opposite meaning.

As ever, her engagements were carefully laid out and detailed for her and she had no control over them. She wanted to cancel the week's events, take time out, not have to shake hands, read speeches or even smile! But there was no way that was going to happen. There were too many people to keep happy or at least have a good attempt at doing so.

Friday evening eventually came, and Jacqui was driven home, mayoral ribbons flapping on the bonnet of the freshly spruced up, shiny black limo. She listened to the Chauffeur talking but didn't hear what he said – it was all a miserable, heavy blur and Jacqui realised it wasn't for the first time. A combination of Jacqui's tiredness and the soft, purring sound of the Jaguar engine saw Jacqui fall asleep and was startled to be woken by her Chauffeur

'Madam we've arrived' he called releasing the driver's seatbelt and moving out of the car to the rear to open the rear door where Jacqui was seated.

Jacqui was startled to be woken and was embarrassed to realise that she had fallen asleep.

'Oh, thank you Mark. Sorry I was snoozing. I don't know why I ….'

'It's fine Madam. Have a restful evening and I will surely see you tomorrow'.

It had rained all week, and Jacqui meandered around the wet puddles in her garden up to the front door of her house, waving to the Chauffeur to confirm he was free to drive away. She thought about Peter's words to her last night when he had wearily, yet hopefully, asked:

'Jacqui, darling, do you think things will change? You look so sad'. Those words had surprised her as Peter didn't usually analyse her in such depth. It had made her feel uneasy.

Continuing to avoid the puddles she moved up to the front of the house, the front room window and porch both brightly lit. Before she had chance to take the set of house keys out of her large, soft dark leather bag Peter opened the door.

'Turn round' he said firmly and pointed her to his waiting car, on the driveway. Peter's car was usually parked in the garage but today it looked ready for a quick getaway, facing the road with a set of bags clearly visible through the back window. Puzzled, Jacqui looked up at Peter's smiling face

'We're going away' he said firmly as he tuned to the car 'and it's not optional, Mrs Mayor'. Jacqui frowned. She hated it when Peter called her by that name, she felt he was being sarcastic and was sending some sort of subliminal message that she was wedded to her role rather than him. She felt tears welling in her eyes, steaming her glasses up. She must call her office to explain that she would be away, to almost ask for time out. She told herself to get a perspective as he led her to the car.

Peter drove them at speed to the airport. Perhaps this break, wherever they were going and for however long would help her feel better, like the old self that she longed to be. Maybe it would bring them closer together again. Looking at Peter, she truly ached for that to be the case.

Peter had not planned his preferred and usual itinerary-led holiday. This time he had realised that they needed to go with the flow, do what Jacqui wanted, be content with last minute decisions and to be prepared for several changes of mind. That was what Jacqui needed he had assured himself.

He was right and at the end of each day Jacqui had told Peter 'The day has been amazing, restful. I feel so much happier'. She had enjoyed the daily choosing of sites to see, where to shop, lazy moments by the pool and deciding on which foods to eat.

'I'm so sorry tomorrow will be our last day' Jacqui whispered, looking at Peter as they shared a late-night cocktail at the poolside. 'Where has the time gone? I feel so refreshed and yet I

126

would love to stay, stay away'. He looked at her and nodded in quiet agreement.

Jacqui and Peter climbed the waiting aircraft steps, racing to get to the top as quickly as they could. They smiled at one another silently. They were not boarding the return flight home that Peter had originally planned but instead were taking a long-haul flight that they had booked with a mixture of teenage excitement and haste the previous day.

'A new start' whispered Peter to Jacqui as they showed their boarding passes

'One way, no going back' announced Jacqui animatedly to the flight attendant as he showed them to their first-class seats. The Flight Attendant grinned sensing their nervousness.

Was this a new start that they had quietly longed for, they wondered. They giggled as they remembered Jacqui swimming in the pool and emerging lighter than she had felt for a long while and in more ways than one.

'Cheers, Darling' beamed Peter settling down comfortably in his generous sized airline seat. Jacqui responded by chinking her champagne glass against his and sipped the cold, golden sparkling liquid 'Here's to After Sun'.

The pool at the Grand in Paris was re-opened following its sudden closure in the week due to what the manager called 'maintenance requirements'. The mystery of the malfunctioning pool pump had finally been resolved with the eventual retrieval of a clumsy metal chain tangled up in the machinery.

It was made of shiny squares that were far heavier than they looked and was tied with a dark blue ribbon. The hotel staff crowded round to look at the piece, not having seen anything like it before and there was loud, fast chatter among the staff all wondering where it had come from, none of them coming up with an answer.

Suspicion

It was easy to access Room 317.

Sheila just smiled sweetly at the young chambermaid, explained that she was meeting her husband later, but needed to leave a surprise gift for him in the room. She even produced an email from the Hotel confirming an overnight stay in his name, John Harding.

The chambermaid was reassured by this and opened the door with her pass key.

Sheila thanked her and entered.

The room was pleasant enough for a typical Hotel. Utility furniture, shower but no bath. Small table and a single chair, sliding mirror doors with a hanging rail and a three-door unit. Strange how she needed to know mundane details like this, but it was important to her as she tried to build a picture of her husband's secret life.

She sat on the bed, opened her shopping bag, took out the urn and placed it, together with a handwritten letter, on the bedside table. Then she went over the events of the past few weeks in her mind.

The sudden death of her husband had been a great shock. They had a happy, loving marriage for over thirty years or so she had thought.

It was only when she was going through his personal belongings after the funeral, that she discovered the awful truth. John, her devoted husband had been having an affair.

It was a shock she still couldn't comprehend. John was the last person anyone could imagine having an affair. He was a 'Steady Eddy' type, quiet and unassuming, even boring.

Until she read the email confirming the Hotel booking in the private diary in which he had recorded meetings every 6 weeks with M. And finally, the handwritten letter from Margaret, thanking him for the wonderful evening spent together. Sheila had to accept the fact that her husband had been unfaithful, not once but repeatedly, for how long she would never know.

Whilst, she felt a deep sense of betrayal, as though the past thirty years had meant nothing to him, this betrayal eclipsed all the love she had felt for him. She came to a decision. His ashes should be with this Margaret, as she obviously meant more to him than she did.

So, she wrote a letter, sealed it, and took it, together with the urn, to the Hotel. For Margaret. She hoped it would be as much a shock to Margaret as it had been to her, still struggling to cope with his death and infidelity.

The letter said,

'Dear Margaret,

I hope this will come as much of a shock to you, as the discovery of my husband's unfaithfulness was to me, after learning of your affair, following his sudden death. The urn contains his ashes, I feel that their rightful place is with you.

I shall be waiting for you in the foyer.

Mrs Sheila Harding'

She felt better after this, and, braced herself for the upcoming confrontation. She settled into a large comfortable armchair, positioned directly in front of the lift, and waited expectantly. It was late afternoon now, so she ordered a small whisky from the bar.

There were very few single ladies leaving the lift, certainly no one who looked anything like a scarlet woman, not that Sheila had much idea of what a scarlet woman should look like.

A little old lady approached her. 'Mrs Harding?' she enquired in a soft voice.

Sheila responded, puzzled. 'Yes. Can I help you….?

'I am Margaret ', came the response.

Sheila was confused.

This could surely not be the woman her husband had been having an affair with. A little old lady probably approaching 80 years of age. Margaret, whilst smartly dressed, needed a walking stick to help her, and it was obvious that there was no possibility of John having an affair with her, unless it involved whips, and leather…. Sheila shuddered at the thought.

Seeing the confusion in Sheila's face, Margaret continued. 'I think I owe you an explanation.

First of all, may I say how terribly sorry I am to learn of your husband's sudden death. John was a wonderful man and has been so kind to me since the death of my husband, Harry.

Let me reassure you from the start, there has never been anything improper in our relationship.'

Sheila's face softened as she began to realise that she had perhaps been too quick to judge.

'I met John, your husband, when he was a young man and joined my husband's firm. As you know, John came from a troubled childhood. Abandoned as a young child, he ended up in an orphanage. He applied for a job at the age of 16, and although he had no formal qualifications, Harry saw something in him. Harry too had a difficult upbringing, so understood how difficult it was to escape one's background when orphaned.

John worked with Harry who took a fatherly interest in his welfare and his development. We had no children of our own, you see. And it was a source of great pride to Harry when John progressed up through the business, entirely on his own merits, to become Sales Director.

Sadly, in his later years, Harry developed Alzheimer's, but rather than ignoring him and leaving us both to cope alone, John took a real interest in Harry's welfare, taking him out and giving me some respite from the 24/7 care that Harry needed.

The one stipulation John made was that no one should know of his kindness to both of us.

This continued till Harry's death and didn't stop there. John continued to keep an eye on me, taking out to dinner every six weeks, and paying for me to stay over before taking me home the next day.

John has been a wonderful friend to us both, and I'm only sorry that he didn't share this with you, whatever his reasons, I guess.'

Sheila felt a huge sense of relief, coupled with shame that she had ever doubted her husband.

'I'm so sorry Sheila'.

Tears welled up and the two women just clung to each other, words being unnecessary.

'I'm so glad to have met you Margaret,' said Sheila.

'Finding out how kind John has been to you and your husband, I feel ashamed for ever having suspected him of being unfaithful. It's such a relief'.

'I understand', said Margaret, giving her new friend a heartfelt squeeze.

As they said their goodbyes, Sheila didn't notice the beautiful redhead with the long legs sitting at the bar, sipping a champagne cocktail, checking her watch every five minutes.

Family Values

Alex hadn't been back to the village for over two years. He still remembered the day he had left as though it was yesterday. It had been a Wednesday in November, the first of the Christmas markets was in full swing and the sky was heavy with snow that was stalking the village, circling overhead waiting to unleash its full fury. A day later and Alex would have been snowed in, trapped with the anger, the accusations and worst of all the betrayal in the eyes of his family.

Billy had taken it the hardest, begging him not to go with the innocence of a 12-year-old who simply didn't understand why there was a problem.

Now two years later, as he stepped outside the station the familiarity of the village hit him with full force. The smell from the bakery, the barking from the dog groomers and the neon 'open' sign in the late-night convenience store were exactly as they had been when he had left. As he stood taking in the familiar sights and sounds it felt to Alex that he was the only thing that had changed and that made him nervous.

Wrapping his scarf more tightly round his neck and lifting his head up high he set off towards his daughter's house, pulling his suitcase behind him. He was tempted to go to his cottage first. He knew Geoff his neighbour had put the heating on and left some basic provisions in the kitchen, but he knew he needed to get the meeting over with as soon as possible. If word got out that he was back and he hadn't gone straight to Hannah's it could shatter the fragile peace that had been brokered through letters and phone calls over the last six months.

It had been hard talking through his decisions and he could see Hannah's point of view. She had lived in the village all her life, it was a small tight knit community.

Everyone had rallied round Alex when his wife, Hannah's mum had died, and he couldn't have managed to finish raising her without their support.

It was also a very traditional place to live. The church was still very much the centre of village life and any deviation from its conservative values was met with strong opposition. There were no lad mags on display in the newsagents, no late-night bars, and an attempt by the two newcomers to set up an LGBGTQ support group had been squashed pretty quickly.

Alex really did understand why his choices had been hard for Hannah to accept, and it would probably be easier for her if he hadn't come back, but Alex missed his grandson Billy too much to stay away. He had adored Billy from the moment he was born. He had missed two years of Billy's life and didn't want to miss any more precious time.

Alex paused at Hannah's gate trying to push away the memories of the last time he had been here. The anger and hurt had felt too much to bear but at 62 years of age Alex knew this was his last chance to be who he really was. He braced himself then marched up the path and rang the bell.

Hannah had been waiting, nerves jangling and stomach churning, not knowing how this was going to work out. She opened the door and took in the sight of her father.

Auburn hair in a chic bob, subtle makeup highlighting his large brown eyes and high cheekbones. A well-fitting dusky pink jacket complimented a pair of burgundy pants and black knee length boots.

'Hello Dad, or do I have to call you Alex now?'

'Call me Dad, I will always be your dad no matter what I wear' said Alex as he lingered uncertainly on the step.

Suddenly, thundering down the stairs came Billy, with all the clumsiness of a fourteen-year-old boy.

'You're here. Wow you look amazing. This is so cool, I'm the only kid in my school that has a Trandad. I can call you Trandad can't I?'

As the tension broke and everyone laughed Alex stepped inside. Things might not always be easy, but he had made his return, He was back home where he belonged.

Wander Lust

The doors opened, inviting Diane to proceed as she clung onto the handle of her suitcase doubting each step. Her passport burned in her pocket, having been checked a million times on the journey here. She exhaled slowly and loudly as she took in her surroundings.

The airport was unusually calm, there were barely any passengers, nor was there much noise or any excitement happening. It was a time of transition for staff from those worn out from the night shift handing over to those allowing their coffees to wake them up, applying another coat of lipstick in an attempt to appear bright eyed and ready for their shift.

Diane looked around nervously – it felt clean, organised, almost sterile. The light felt overwhelming after the darkness outside, and she grabbed her sunglasses. They also gave her a chance to hide and feel more inconspicuous. She felt a sense of anticipation. Although shops and cafes were open, there was very little life within them. It felt like a temporary space in a temporary state. A calmness with a promise of much more beyond.

Diane glanced up at the information board knowing it was probably too early for any updates. She'd always had to be organised with two now grown-up kids and a husband who worked away a lot. She winced when she thought of Jeff, guilt rippling through every part of her body. She never thought he'd never be enough for her. Until Marco entered her life.

She ordered herself a double espresso and sat down to savour the bitter taste and enjoy the caffeine buzz. Once the first couple of sips worked their magic Diane began to doubt herself. What was she doing? That was the problem with coffee – after the rush came the uncertainty, the anxieties, and the wondering. Was she doing the right thing?

Just as she was questioning her crazy life choices, her phone beeped. It was Jeff.

'I'll miss you. I love you x'

Her heart dropped. This was the last thing she needed. How could she do this to the man she had loved for so long. Diane glanced back towards the entrance, back to the life she knew and loved; the safety, the warmth, and the happiness.

'What am I doing?' she said aloud and gathered her bag and passport. 'I am not that kind of woman'.

Just then, her phone pinged again. She knew it was him before she even glanced down. 'Darling, I'm waiting for you.'

The familiar longing permeating every pore in her body, her heart accelerating and blood rushing away from her head, all rational thought disappearing. This feeling, along with the effects of the double espresso, made her light-headed and she needed to grab a nearby chair to steady herself.

Oh Marco. This was not supposed to happen.

When Diane had first been commissioned to write the piece about perimenopausal married women looking for something more, she had signed up to the online dating site *extra.com*. Jeff had been supportive and had helped create her online personae, both a male and a female one to interact with both men and women – all in the name of research. For discretion, no photos were shown on this website – users had to request these and then to accept them. This meant that people read each other's profiles rather than just swiping left or right on a photo.

Jeff and Diane pored over profiles together – sending messages to lots of different people. It had really rekindled the romantic side of their relationship, opened channels of communication, and forced them to talk more to each other about what they wanted. It was a lot of fun and Diane had gained a real insight into other people's lives. Diane often thought how lucky she was, Jeff was a wonderful husband.

Now, after steadying herself, Diane 's head continued to spin with the confusion of what she was doing. She hadn't expected any of this, she hadn't meant to reply to Marco's message when Jeff was out of town, had never realised the impact both his words and his photos would have on her.

Marco was unlike all the other men she had chatted to on the website. He sounded open and honest, witty, clever, brave. Messages flowed back and forth between them and before she knew it several hours had passed. At this point she didn't even know what he looked like, but he was certainly saying the right things.

Diane looked up at the departure board, she was able to check in now. But somehow, she felt glued to the spot, with this turmoil in her head struggling to make sense yet, despite all this life was going on around her. The departure hall was waking up, becoming more lively, busier, and louder.

She thought back to when she first clapped eyes on Marco. His handsome, kind, rugged face - the epitome of everything Italian. She'd felt herself holding her breath, unable to fathom if this Adonis was real. There was always the chance on a site like this, that it could be a catfish but when he suggested a video chat there was no denying that this Italian beauty was the real deal.

Their relationship had developed over the past two months, Jeff was away a lot, so it wasn't difficult, and Diane told herself that it was only talking so it wasn't really being unfaithful. But she knew deep down that this was something more and when Jeff was around and she'd made excuses to sneak away just to message or talk to Marco, Diane knew things were getting out of control.

It was time. She needed to check in, but the guilt was paralysing her. She looked down at her booking form folded neatly into her passport. Diane remembered how sure she had felt when Marco suggested that she came over to Milan for the weekend. She hadn't doubted anything then. Diane's feelings and her longing for Marco had overridden any possible guilt she felt about Jeff. But now - how could she risk twenty-five years of marriage? For what? A one-off affair? He was married too for God's sake. It wasn't like she was going to move to Italy.

A huge realisation washed over her. She was a fool. A typical bored middle-aged housewife. An idiot. Stereotypically everything that she was writing about in her article. She needed to stop this before it went any further. Her legs suddenly found movement again and she ran back out of the airport to the taxi rank. Diane was going home.

As she pulled up at the house, she had lived in for the past fifteen years, Diane felt relief. She'd deal with Marco later. Right now, she had to tell Jeff how much she loved him, how he had made her feel like the luckiest woman in the world, and she was sorry that she had never told him enough.

With tears stinging her eyes, she opened the door. The house was quiet – it was still early, and she imagined that he'd still be in bed.
'Jeff!' she shouted up the stairs. She smiled. That man could sleep through anything.

Just then, the door opened behind her. Diane turned round, surprised to see that her husband had been out already.
He didn't notice her at first and he looked happy and excited. But his grin soon turned from ecstasy to torment once he spotted Diane.
'What....?' He stuttered.

As she looked over his shoulder, it didn't take Diane long to realise, Jeff was not alone. She even recognised her as one of the women they had chatted to on the site.
Diane felt the colour drain from her face. She glanced pitifully at the man she had shared a bed with for the past twenty-five years who was now unable to meet her gaze, his eyes staring, shamefully downwards towards the floor.

'Sorry, I err forgot something' she said, grabbed her things and headed out the door, brushing past the curvy blonde lady and wondering if she would still have time to make her flight.

Now or Never

'It's now or never,' said Sue.

Six faces stared back at her, their expressions ranging from blank to incredulous.

Sue had spent the last two years trying to get some meaningful work out of this rag tag bunch of scribes. They had talked about publishing a book of short stories to raise money for the library. Sue realised early on that they talked a good story but trying to get them to put pen to paper was like wading through treacle. She finally had some funding in place and needed to get things moving.

'I really don't think we are ready 'said Jim, leaning back in his chair and folding his arms 'I don't work well under pressure'. His soft lilting accent was at odds with the steely glint in his eyes.

'I'm sorry Sue' whined Helen I've such a lot going on I can't get focussed, so it's a never from me' She threw her pen down and reached for a piece of cake which was, after all, what she came for. Alison looked at her with pity. Didn't Helen realise how much cake she could buy in six weeks for thirty pounds if she just stayed at home? That seemed to give Alison an idea and she started scribbling in her notebook.

'Look Sue, getting undercover in a county lines drug gang has been really tricky and I'm not about to blow my cover for your stupid deadline' snapped Tony. I gave you a story about Nelly, you will just have to run with that.

Sue turned to Tori, a hopeful look on her face. Tori shifted uncomfortably in her seat.

'Well, I did send you six stories last week. But over the weekend the heroine from story one had an affair with the bloke in story three. The kid in story six found out he was adopted, and his real parents were the couple in story two, except they aren't both his parents as she had an affair with the man in story five who is his real dad. It's going to be a few weeks until I sort this mess out, so I won't make the deadline I'm afraid'.

Knowing he was next in the firing line, the group were surprised to see Kazik starting to rock backwards and forwards in his chair, and large tears start to run down his face.

Linda, the most thoughtful writer in the group gently touched his arm. 'Kazik, whatever is wrong?

Kazik tried to control the sobs that were wracking his body. 'It's my mother, Sue,' he gasped, 'she wants me to write. My whole life she has tried to make me into a writer, and I can't do it. I want to be a dancer and a florist, and she can't accept it'.

Linda, sensing story prompt gold, tried to commiserate with one eye on Kazik while frantically trying to scribble down a quick story outline…. mother, dancing, son, and flowers. She would go back to this outline three months later and would be puzzled. Nevertheless, she would write a story about a mother who would dance in the sun wearing a garland of flowers.

Sue had heard enough. She stood up and stumbled backwards into the whiteboard.

'Oh, my knees' she groaned.

'Knees my backside' muttered Jim. The group smirked; they had all seen the gin in her handbag.

Sue went into the computer room in search of Stan and some solace, but he wasn't there. She spotted a note with her name on stuck to one of the computer screens.

'Dear Sue, all these months I have been forced to sit on my own while you talk about 'writerly' things. Well, I've done more than provide tea and cake with my time. I've used it to pen my first novel. Who would have thought the tea boy would be the only one to have it in him? My advance from Harper Collins hit my bank account this morning and I'm off to Marrakesh to write a sequel. 'Toodles Dahlings'. Stan'

This time, Sue's knees really did give way.

Milton Keynes UK
Ingram Content Group UK Ltd.
UKHW021143110724
445379UK00012BC/289